Power, Platforms & Participation

By Mayada El-Zoghbi

Foreword by Payal Dalal,
Global Executive in Social Impact and Philanthropy

Elevation
Publishing Group, LLC.

Published by **Elevation Publishing Group, LLC.**
Cover design by **DeVasha Lloyd**

eBook ISBN: 979-8-9999460-0-3
Paperback ISBN: 979-8-9999460-2-7
Hardcover ISBN: 979-8-9999460-1-0

Printed in United States of America

Table of Content

Foreword...1

Chapter 1: The Digital Economy.......................................4

Chapter 2: The Digital Divide...15

Chapter 3: Gateway to the Digital Economy: Digital Finance..........33

Chapter 4: An Inclusive Digital Economy..........................52

Chapter 5: Countering Entitlement & Backlash 63

Chapter 6: Inclusion is Good for Business........................77

Chapter 7: Equal access to opportunity............................91

Chapter 8: Limiting Digital Monopolies 102

Chapter 9: Leveling the Playing Field 115

Chapter 10: Development Cooperation 130

Chapter 11: Civil Society 148

Chapter 12: The Race to Rebalance Power 157

Chapter 13: Closing 174

Foreword

By Payal Dalal,
Global Executive in Social Impact and Philanthropy

We live in a world where technology can amplify opportunity or entrench inequality. Nowhere is this tension more visible than in the rapidly expanding digital economy – the fabric which connects individuals, businesses and data in an intricate network of value creation, innovation and exchange. *Power, Platforms & Participation* is a timely, compelling and easy-to-read exploration of the forces shaping this new economic frontier and, more importantly, a guide to ensuring that it works for everyone.

This book arrives at a crucial moment. It takes a complex topic - the intersection of technology, finance and inclusion - and translates it into clear, practical guidance that deepens understanding and sparks ideas for real world collaboration. Whether you're an entrepreneur, policymaker, development practitioner or simply someone curious about the digital age, you'll find yourself both informed and empowered by its insights.

At the heart of this book is a powerful message: access to the digital economy is no longer a luxury. It's a necessity. From basic financial transactions to entrepreneurs reaching new customers and managing inventory, to governments delivering social benefit payments, the digital economy is not just reshaping *how* people connect - but also determining *who* gets to be connected.

I've seen this transformation firsthand. Through the support of the Mastercard Center for Inclusive Growth and RISE, Champi, a 24-year-old garment worker in Cambodia, began receiving her wages digitally instead of in cash. With basic financial education and a safe place to receive her digital wages, she started saving each month and now feels more secure about her family's future. "If someone is sick, then I have savings to pay the hospital bill," she says. Stories like Champi's show how digital access can unlock opportunity, build resilience and bring more people into the formal economy. That is the promise and the imperative of digital inclusion.

But access remains uneven. Too many people are still being left out. *Power, Platforms & Participation* addresses this reality head-on. It unpacks the risks of digital exclusion and growing digital divides - gender, racial, geographic - and goes beyond diagnosing the problem, to offering promising, practical pathways forward. It highlights examples of how technology is already being used to monitor and manage risks - like scams, fraud and exclusionary algorithms - while pointing to solutions that prioritize safety and inclusivity.

It also holds actors accountable. From governments, private sector companies, civil society and global development organizations, everyone plays a role. In today's volatile economic and geopolitical landscape, we know that partnership is more important than ever. As the world navigates mounting headwinds, from economic instability to global conflict and rising inequality, no one can drive digital inclusion alone, and no one can afford to ignore it.

The good news is that inclusion is not just the right thing to do, it's good for business. Inclusion drives innovation, unlocks opportunity and strengthens economies – and *Power, Platforms & Participation* tells that story.

My vision for the digital economy is one where power is shared. Where innovation includes more voices, and where participation is not determined by where you were born, your gender or the color of your skin. *Power, Platforms & Participation* helps us move toward that vision, reminding us that digital tools are powerful, but that power comes with responsibility and accountability.

This message is bought to life by its author, Mayada El-Zoghbi. Few people are better positioned to write this book. With over two decades of leadership in economic development, inclusive finance and market systems, she brings a rare combination of intellectual rigor, practical experience and global perspective. I have had the privilege of watching Mayada in action, as a researcher who leads with the hard questions and as an advisor whose guidance has shaped programs and organizations around the world. In each of these roles, Mayada has carried an unwavering commitment to building systems that serve everyone, and this shines in every chapter of *Power, Platforms & Participation*. This book is not just informed by her experience; it is shaped by her belief in the transformative potential of inclusion.

I admire that this book ties many threads together – digital finance as the gateway and civil society, private sector and public institutions as disruptors and architects of fair, competitive and safe digital economies. It also keeps a focus on concrete solutions, offering a hopeful, grounded vision on how digital systems can serve everyone, not just those already connected.

I hope you take its message to heart, and more importantly, that you take its ideas into action.

Chapter 1

The Digital Economy

I moved to Amsterdam in 2024. It's a city I visited many times as a tourist, and where I met my husband in 2008. The city reminded me of what New York used to be – a lot of local neighborhood stores, people from all around the world, and a place where counterculture dominates. One of the first things I do in a new city is take public transportation. Cash isn't accepted in Amsterdam on public transport, so you need a credit card, e-wallet, or to purchase a pre-paid card for public transportation.

The next thing I had to do was obtain my legal residency. This required getting something called DigiD, a system used by all government agencies, the banking system, and other relevant services to authenticate one's identity. To get a local sim card, I had to have a local bank account. And to get a local bank account, I had to have the DigiD app on my smartphone. In every step of the process to become a resident of this city, I had to interact with the digital economy. My experience, I am sure, is not unique or limited to the city of Amsterdam.

*****

Whether it's paying for coffee at a café, getting on the tram or metro, or ordering clothes or food online, it's nearly impossible to function in today's society without engaging with the digital economy. Everything around us is being digitized, and we must engage with it to get the services we need.

The digital economy refers to activities that are powered by digital technologies. These include the internet, mobile devices, and data-driven processes. Most often, we think about the digital economy as consisting of new businesses like e-commerce giants, or old businesses like banks now offering digital financial services, or tech companies offering cloud services or AI solutions.

But if you look around, you see that the digital economy entails more than commercial or economic activities, but also touches on basic services that any citizen requires from their government, whether that is getting a national identity card, a driver's license, unemployment benefits, social security or pension benefits. Most countries require residents to access government services by first going online to download forms, registering their demand, or making a payment for a service. Today, it's nearly impossible to engage with a government or commercial service by walking into an office and interacting with an agent and getting your service directly. In my first week in Amsterdam, I mistakenly went to the ABN Amro branch in the center of the city to get help opening a bank account. I wasn't even able to make an appointment at the branch and was instructed to do everything online.

Digital development is a priority in many countries

Many governments have digital development plans aimed at leveraging technology to improve public services, enhance connectivity, and drive economic growth. The UK has a Digital Development Strategy (2024-2030), which focuses on inclusivity, security, and sustainability in digital transformation. It addresses challenges such as AI for development, digital public infrastructure, and digital sustainability. Many developing countries are also adopting digital development plans. Digital Egypt 2030 is one such example.

It is a strategy to modernize the economy, improve public services through e-government, e-health, and e-education, and most importantly, it aims to reposition Egypt within the African continent as a leader in the digital age.[1] The strategy focuses on core digital infrastructure (5G networks, fiber optics, and data centers), advancing technological skills and services (IT skills, support for tech start-ups), and a connected society. Within the 38 OECD countries, half of them have dedicated digital development ministries that designed their digital strategies.[2]

Perhaps no country epitomizes the concept of a digital economy more than China. The country has one of the most advanced digital economies in the world, and it's been growing at an exponential rate since 2013. The backbone of the economy is China's leadership in 5G infrastructure and the country's use of data. E-commerce and mobile payments have seen the most aggressive growth in the digital economy, with companies such as JD.com and Alibaba. Digital payments are critical components that facilitate e-commerce and the digital economy, and one of the world's largest players is Ant Group, which runs Alipay, a critical payment platform that drives e-commerce and the digital economy.

Underpinning China's digitalization model is its strategy, *Digital China*. The goal is "a digitally transformed socialist system with Chinese characteristics to demonstrate its superiority over Western developmental models. To succeed, *Digital China* must be both deeply transformative and deeply competitive, the two defining features of its domestic and international missions."[3] China was one of the first countries to issue a digital currency, the e-CNY, or digital yuan. It is a digital currency issued by the People's Bank of China (PBOC) and distributed by commercial banks and payment providers.

---

[1] AEDIC. *Digital Egypt 2030: The strategy that will transform Egypt into a global technology hub* (AEDIC, February 2025).
[2] OECD. *OECD Digital Economy Outlook 2024 (Volume 2): Strengthening Connectivity, Innovation and Trust*, OECD Publishing, Paris (OECD, 2024).
[3] Dorman, David, Digital *China: No Other Digital Strategy Is Anything Like It,* Digital China Wins the Future (June 2021).

What makes an economy digital?

The user touchpoints that I mentioned for my experience in Amsterdam are just the tip of the iceberg of what it means to be a digital economy. Researchers have been looking at what's beneath the water -- what does it mean to make an economy digital. Digital Planet at Tufts University has identified several enablers and tracks them.

They identified four areas that interact and together can determine just how digitalized an economy may be. They use these areas to then measure economies around the globe and then map them based on where they are in their journey. The four areas they look at are:

Supply conditions. The Tufts researchers define these as the existing digital and logistical infrastructure that enables transactions to happen and firms to deliver on their services. They include things like communications technology, payments technology and transportation infrastructure, and logistics.

Demand conditions. These are defined as the profile of the population using the services and whether they are already capable and interested in digital goods. They include the skills and desires of the consumer base, the degree to which these consumers have smartphones and digital accounts, and how deep or inclusive this demand is. Inclusion refers to who is able to access it and whether it's only in the cities and misses rural communities, or if it's only among certain segments and excludes others.

Institutional environment. This is defined as the legal environment and the policy enablers that encourage both demand and supply conditions, including things like taxation policies, investor protections, and processes for business registration. More basic rules of law, transparency, and trust are also fundamental to a well-functioning digital economy.

Innovation and change. This refers to the ease by which companies can create value, attract talent, and attract capital. It also involves the ecosystem for research.

7

Digital Planet developed an index that plots 90 economies according to their digital readiness. They define *standout* economies as those that are highly digital already and have continued momentum to grow; *breakout* economies refer to those that have momentum but are not yet as fully digitalized; *stall-out* economies speaks to those which may be highly digital but exhibit low momentum for continued growth; and *watch out* economies refers to those that are facing challenges toward digital development.

In their latest report (2020), in the *standout* category which captures countries that have strong momentum and advanced digital development, it's not surprising to see South Korea, Singapore, Estonia, the U.S., the UAE, and Qatar. In the *stall-out* category, countries that have high levels of digital development, but have limited momentum, there are countries like the Nordic states, Belgium, and France. The *breakout* category includes many developing economies like Indonesia, Vietnam, India, and Kenya. These have significant momentum for growth but still relatively low digital development. And, finally, in the *watch out* category we have Nigeria, Ethiopia, Brazil, and South Africa. Those countries have neither momentum nor an evolved digital economy. Given that the report is from 2020, it's likely that countries have already made substantial shifts. For example, recently Brazil invested heavily in a digital payments platform called PIX, which is quickly advancing the infrastructure for the digital economy to take off. And even Ethiopia[4] has a digital strategy, although it continues to suffer from poor connectivity.

---

[4] DigWatch, *Digital Ethiopia 2025 Strategy* (DigWatch, May 2020).

Figure 1. Plotting digitalization around the world

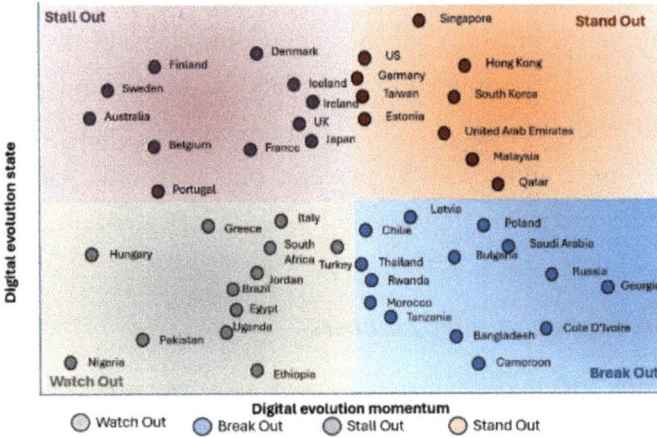

Source: Digital in the Time of Covid: Trust in the Digital Economy and Its Evolution
Across 90 Economies as the Planet Paused for a Pandemic, Tufts University

Is the digital economy good for everyone?

I was probably able to adapt to the digital development of the Netherlands because I came from the United States, where the digitalization journey is mature and where I already had exposure and the capability to use Smart phones, e-wallets, and other digital interfaces. But imagine I had grown up in Egypt instead of the United States, where I was originally born. Egypt is in the *watch out* category, that is, it is not as advanced now, nor does it have momentum for change. Moving to a place like the Netherlands from a place like Egypt for someone in my age category would have probably meant significant hardship. While using a smartphone probably would not have been a problem, using digital payments and the digital identity authentication would likely pose significant challenges for someone in their 50's.

As might be expected, World Bank research shows that trends toward digital development are not benefiting everyone equally. This is both within countries and between countries.

9

For example, while internet use is high in middle-income countries, it is falling behind in low-income countries.

As of 2022, 5.3 billion people were using the internet, but only one in four people in low-income countries were doing so.[5] The divide between countries is best exemplified by the data on broadband penetration. Broadband subscriptions in 2022 were relatively high in high- and middle-income countries at 30 percent, but were only 4.4 percent in lower-middle income countries and only 0.5 percent in low-income countries.

Women are lagging in some countries

India is one of the countries leading the way in building digital infrastructure. It has invested in what is known as the 'India Stack,' which is a set of foundational technologies consisting of digital IDs (Aadhaar), a digital payment system (Unified Payments Interface), and electronic know your customer protocols (e-KYC). Coupled with policy imperatives to improve women's access to finance and large subsidies to organizations to support women to register for national IDs and bank accounts, India has seen very significant progress in addressing some aspects of the digital divide. Over 282 million women[6] now have bank accounts in their names, which matches the same rate as men. Digital IDs are nearly universal for Indian women. While these are very important steps, the digital divide persists, and the economic benefits of this digital access has not yet reached women.

India has the widest gender digital divide compared to countries in the Asia Pacific region. Internet access is particularly low, with only 15 percent of women in India actively using the internet, a rate much lower than that of their male counterparts.

---

[5] World Bank Group, *Digital Progress an Development Report 2023* (World Bank, 2023).
[6] https://pmjdy.gov.in/account

On the technology access point, only 25 percent of women in India own a mobile phone (compared to 41 percent of men).[7]

As a result, the digital economy has yet to translate into meaningful economic benefits for women. Women's workforce participation at 32.8 percent remains far below the global average of 47 percent.[8] This lag is often attributable to many other constraints that can't easily be explained by only economic analysis. Women in India face many other constraints that need to be addressed including familial support, safe mobility, discrimination and harassment in the workplace, and broader societal expectations.

Recent data from the Time Use Survey in India shows just how societal expectations and in turn, choices by women affect their ability to invest in employment. Once married, women's unpaid chores increase to 27 percent of their time. Time for employment and learning declines considerably from 23 percent of their time before marriage to only 6 percent of their time, whereas it stays the same for men.

[7] Times of India, *Gender inequality and the digital divide in India* (Times of India, July 1, 2023).
[8] Ministry of Labor and Employment, *Female Labour Utilization in India* (Ministry of Labor and Employment of India, April 2023).

Figure 2: Time usage before and after marriage in India
Women versus men

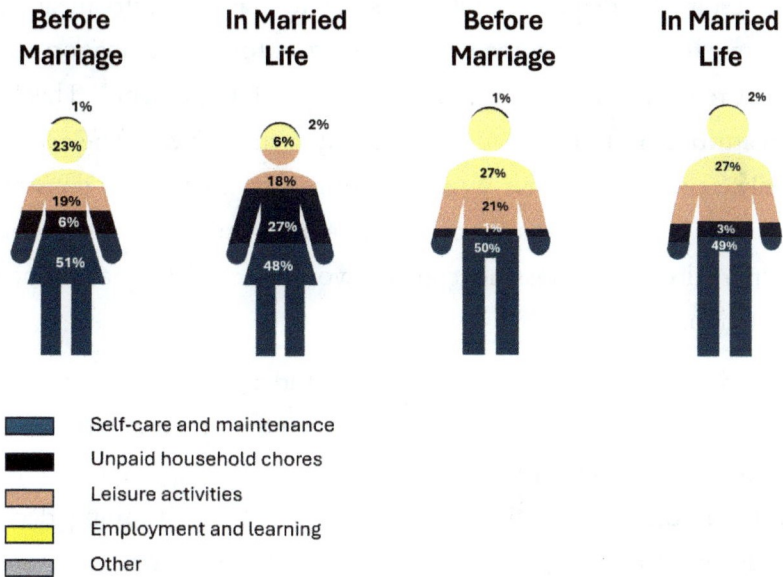

Before Marriage	In Married Life	Before Marriage	In Married Life

Legend:
- Self-care and maintenance
- Unpaid household chores
- Leisure activities
- Employment and learning
- Other

Source: LiveMint, 28 May 2025

A digital economy has fewer opportunities for low-income people in rural communities

China has one of the most digitally connected economies in the world, extending to rural communities. To reach rural segments, China has included widespread adoption of satellite remote sensing, AI, and the Internet of Things (IOT), and in turn investments in precision sowing, intelligent irrigation, and AI informed fertilizer application. The use of online commerce by rural households has also shown an increase. Online sales of agricultural goods increased by nearly 35 percent in 2022. All in all, there is evidence of increased digital production, marketing, and integrating digital channels in existing supply chains.

And yet the benefits of this digitalization have yet to reach everyone in rural communities. Researchers indicate that the potential for digital connectivity is more apt for non-agricultural work. It's particularly relevant for entrepreneurs, online learners, and skills building for higher-educated and higher-income groups.

While it does have some benefits for rural households, particularly for non-agriculture labor, evidence shows that digitalization is increasing the digital divide within rural communities.[9]

The main drivers of this digital divide are linked to beginning endowments and skills of households. Households with limited education and skills will not see the value of investing in technology. This makes it less likely that these households are able to exploit off-farm opportunities such as trade or e-commerce. Those who are already better educated are more likely to invest in technology and are thus more likely to diversify their households away from agriculture and into non-agricultural employment; they are also more likely to invest in learning online. The net effect is that there is a widening income gap between high-income and low-income households in rural areas.[10]

Figure 3: Income growth trends in rural China 2002-2022

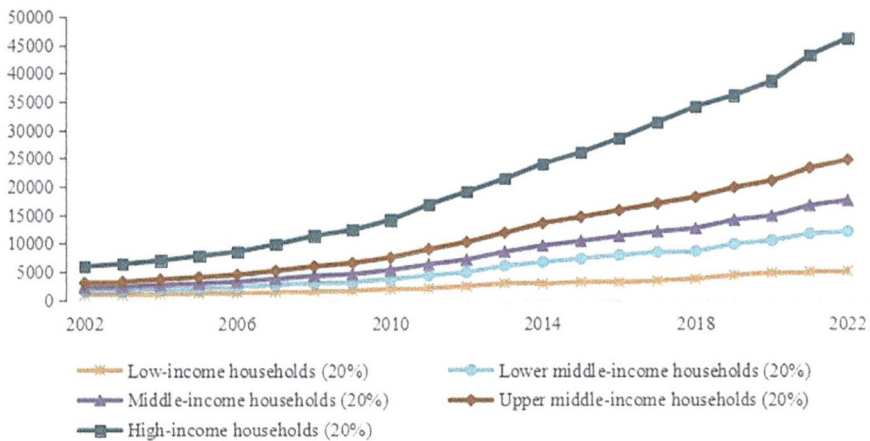

Source: Wang, H., Leng, H. & Yuan, M. From opportunity to inequality: how the rural digital economy shapes intra-rural income distribution (Humanit Soc Sci Commun 12, 534, 2025).

---

[9] Wang, H., Leng, H. & Yuan, M. *From opportunity to inequality: how the rural digital economy shapes intra-rural income distribution*. (Humanit Soc Sci Commun 12, 534, 2025).
[10] ibid

How do we ensure the benefits extend to all groups in society?

Awareness is a big part of the answer. But it's obviously not enough. In each country, region, and society, we must start with understanding who will benefit and who will not. Once we understand that, we shift our focus to understanding the specific barriers that different groups face. The solutions are not always obvious.

This book is intended to provide a broad overview of what needs to happen for everyone to benefit from the digital economy. We will cover the groups in society who are most likely to be excluded from the digital economy (Chapter 2). We will then delve into one of the most important gateways into the digital economy, the financial sector (Chapter 3). We'll then shift to what it means to be inclusive in the digital economy (Chapter 4). Given the historical moment we are in, we can't discuss inclusion without also discussing how those who have been historically privileged may create a backlash as benefits are distributed (Chapter 5). In the last section of the book, we shift toward solutions.

We'll start with why inclusion is not only good as a social good, but also financially beneficial for business (Chapter 6).

We'll focus on what governments need to do to address the unique monopolistic power of data-based business models (Chapter 7), then we'll discuss broader policy and regulatory solutions (Chapter 8). We'll discuss what equal access actually means for all groups and how to increase uptake and usage of digital technologies (Chapter 9). Then we'll discuss the role of development cooperation to support low-capacity governments to keep up with the digital revolution (Chapter 10); we'll discuss the role of civil society (Chapter 11), and finally we'll address other important solutions for rebalancing the power dynamics away from tech companies to consumers (Chapter 12). The last chapter briefly touches on recent developments and offers a view of why changes toward a more equitable digital economy may be within reach (Chapter 13).

Chapter 2
The Digital Divide

In 2016, this article ran in Al Jazeera:

India: Banning women from owning mobile phones

Villages in the western state of Gujarat are barring girls and unmarried women from having phones to help with studies.

26 Feb 2016

Several villages in western India have banned girls and single women from owning mobile phones, saying the devices distract them from their studies.

Villages in the Mehsana and Banaskantha districts in Gujarat state imposed the ban, and more villages have joined the campaign, said Ranjit Singh Thakor, president of the Mehsana district council.

The ban applies to girls under the age of 18 and unmarried women, he said.[11]

Source: Al Jazeera

There are 2.7 billion people who are not connected to the internet. The reasons are multifold: availability, affordability, gender norms, digital literacy, among many other issues.[12]

---

[11] Al Jazeera, *India banning women from owning mobile phones,* (Al Jazeera, February 26, 2016).
[12] Internet Society

The digital divide is the gap between those who have access to the internet and the means of accessing it, such as computers and mobile phones, and those who are not connected.[13] Given that increasingly work, information, and opportunities are mediated through the internet, this lack of access and the means to access it (computers or mobile devices), prevents many people from engaging meaningfully in the digital age and the digital economy.

While there are many groups excluded, the biggest gap exists between men and women. Worldwide, men are 21 percent more likely to be online than women.[14] The biggest gap is in South Asia, followed by Sub-Saharan Africa. The gap is smallest in North America, East Asia, Europe, and the Middle East and North Africa (MENA). In MENA, despite the relatively small digital divide, it has not translated into the many benefits expected with digital technologies, such as increased employment and entrepreneurship.

Figure 1: Worldwide, men are 21% more likely to be online than women
Comparison of the % of women and men online in different regions of the world

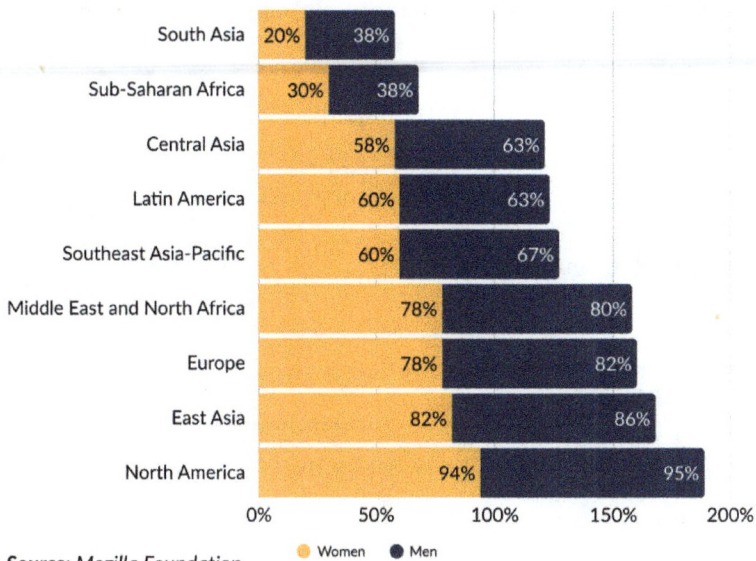

Region	Women	Men
South Asia	20%	38%
Sub-Saharan Africa	30%	38%
Central Asia	58%	63%
Latin America	60%	63%
Southeast Asia-Pacific	60%	67%
Middle East and North Africa	78%	80%
Europe	78%	82%
East Asia	82%	86%
North America	94%	95%

Source: Mozilla Foundation

---

[13] Mozilla Foundation
[14] ibid

Mobile phones – gateway to the internet and development outcomes

Today, more people access the internet through their mobile phones than through computers (55 percent versus 42 percent).[15] Thus, owning a mobile phone is likely to remain the most important gateway to participating in the digital economy. Ownership of technology, particularly mobile phones, correlates with greater outcomes, including higher consumption, estimated at 16-24 percent higher than those without phones.[16] The benefits of phone ownership also extend to safety in the community, access to information, and staying connected to family and friends. Phones also unlock another important door, access to the financial system.

Increasingly, financial services are delivered through mobile phones, which enable women to save, pay bills, and borrow with limited engagement outside the home.[17]

According to GSMA, women were on a path to catch up with men with regard to mobile phone access, but in 2022 the pace of progress slowed down for a second year in a row. As of 2022, men were 17 percent more likely to have access to smartphones than women. While 67 percent of men globally have access to smartphones, only 55 percent of women do.[18]

The Al Jazeera story at the beginning of this chapter points to some of the most intransigent obstacles — social and gender norms — that keep many women and girls from taking the first step into the digital economy by owning mobile phones.

---

[15] Badalyan, Albert, *Mobile vs desktop internet usage statistic* (DigitalSilk, June 19, 2025).

[16] Roessler, P., et al. *Mobile-phone ownership increases poor women's household consumption: A field experiment in Tanzania* (ICRW, May 2018).

[17] Kabir, R., & Klugman, J. *Women's financial inclusion in a digital world: How mobile phones can reduce gender gaps* (Georgetown Institute for Women, Peace and Security, 2019).

[18] *GSMA, Mobile Gender Gap Report (GSMA, 2023).*

The perception that phones distract girls from their studies or that phones provide access for women to cheat on their husbands or a myriad of other beliefs are ultimately what gets in the way, even when mobile phones are made accessible and affordable.

Connectivity comes next

In developing countries, the gap between men and women's access to mobile internet — accessing the internet through a mobile phone — remains unchanged at 19 percent which equates to 310 million fewer women accessing the internet than men.[19]

Figure 2: Gender gap in mobile internet use in LMICs, by region

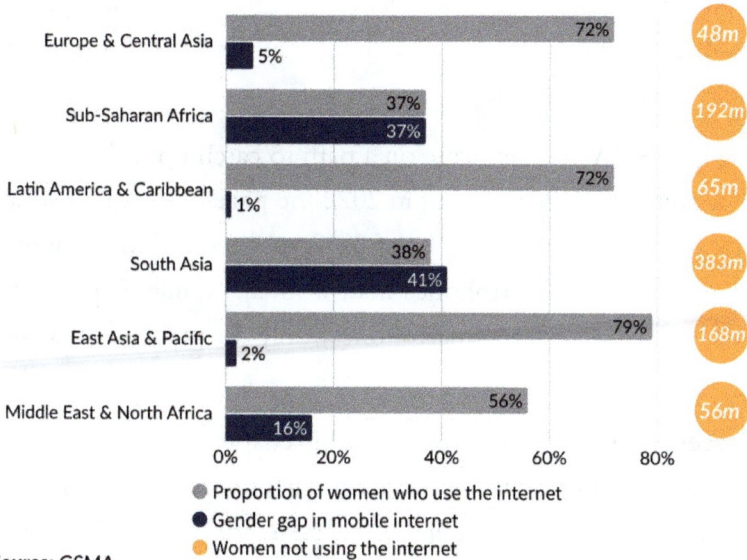

Source: GSMA

There are more than 900 million women who are not using mobile internet in developing countries. Most of these women are in South Asia (383m) and Sub-Saharan Africa (192m).

[19] ibid

The gender gaps in these regions are significantly higher than the global average, 41 percent and 36 percent, respectively. To achieve parity by 2030, more than 100 million more women would need to adopt mobile internet each year.[20]

Constraints to technology access and usage

There are a number of constraints to women's access and usage of digital technology.

Awareness and perceived value. Henry Ford said, "If I had asked people what they wanted, they would have said faster horses." This quote refers to the idea that if someone has never seen something, like cars, for instance, they typically can't imagine how it would benefit them. They are likely only to imagine the world they already inhabit with some minor tweaks.

Thus, if someone has never used the internet, they would have difficulties imagining how it can be used to enhance their life. The monthly price tag of paying for data would also influence the perceived value of the internet. Someone who is barely getting by and needs every extra cent to purchase food or pay for rent is not going to imagine what something like the internet can offer them.

Women are less likely to be aware of mobile internet.[21] And they often do not understand the importance of owning a smartphone. For example, a government program in India distributed free smartphones to women. Women did use smartphones to make calls, and they were active users of WhatsApp, but their usage remained limited. Women faced constraints with limited data and battery life on their phones, and thus were not able to translate phone access into meaningful changes in their income-earning potential or productivity.[22]

---

[20] ibid
[21] GSMA, *Mobile Gender Gap Report* (GSMA, 2023).
[22] Highet, C., Singh, N., & Salman, A., *Can Free Phones Close the Digital Gender Divide?* (CGAP, February 2021).

In Sub-Saharan African, a study looked at offering women a choice between feature phones and smartphones. One year after the distribution of the free phones, the researchers found that nearly one-third of those who received free phones were no longer in possession of these phones. It is likely that women did not see the intrinsic value of the phones. Researchers at Harvard University's Evidence for Policy Design note that the distribution of phones without taking into account prevailing norms is not likely to translate into the outcomes expected or may even lead to negative outcomes at the household level, say, for example, if the spouse sees access to the phone as undermining his authority.[23]

Cost. The cost of phones and data are major constraints to usage, for both men and women. While costs are declining over time, in many regions of the world, the average price of a smartphone remains out of reach.[24] The global average is approximately 25 percent of monthly income, or around $104. However, as the graph below demonstrates, there is a wide variation by region.

The lowest costs are in North America, where smartphones only represent less than 2 percent of monthly income, whereas smartphones go as high as 45 percent of monthly income in SSA. In the least developed countries, they are above 50 percent of monthly income, representing more of a luxury good than a necessity.

---

[23] Barboni, G., Field, E., Pande, R., Rigol, N., Schaner, S., & Troyer Moore, C. *A, Though call: Understanding barriers to and impacts of women's mobile phone adoption in India* (Harvard Kennedy School, Evidence for Policy Design, October 2018).
[24] Alliance for Affordable Internet, *How expensive is a smartphone in different countries?* (Alliance for Affordable Internet, October 2021).

Figure 3: Average cost of smartphones by region
As a percent of monthly income

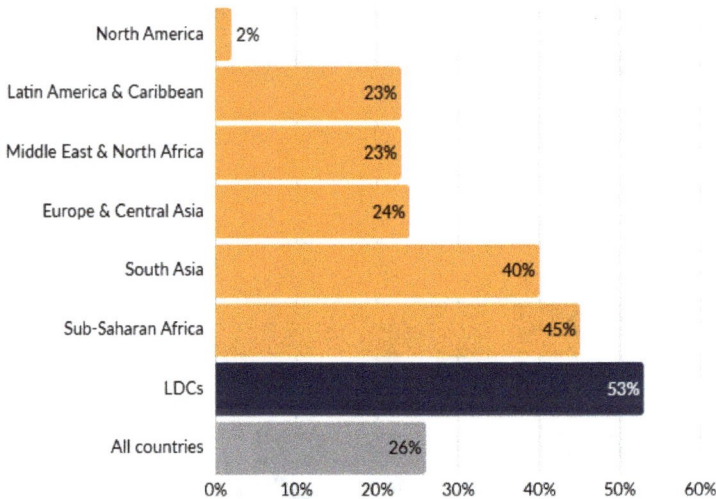

North America	2%
Latin America & Caribbean	23%
Middle East & North Africa	23%
Europe & Central Asia	24%
South Asia	40%
Sub-Saharan Africa	45%
LDCs	53%
All countries	26%

Source: Alliance for Affordable Internet

In addition to the cost of smartphones, the cost of data is also an important constraint, and there is a great deal of variance, even within regions. Figure 4 below depicts the cost of data by sub-region and shows the large variance within different regions in Africa. The price of mobile data varies considerably between northern Africa which is at the lowest end of the spectrum (less than 2 percent of gross monthly income), to Middle Africa where the cost goes as high as 12 percent of gross monthly income for 1 GB of mobile data.

Figure 4: Cost of 1 GB mobile broadband internet

As percent of gross monthly income

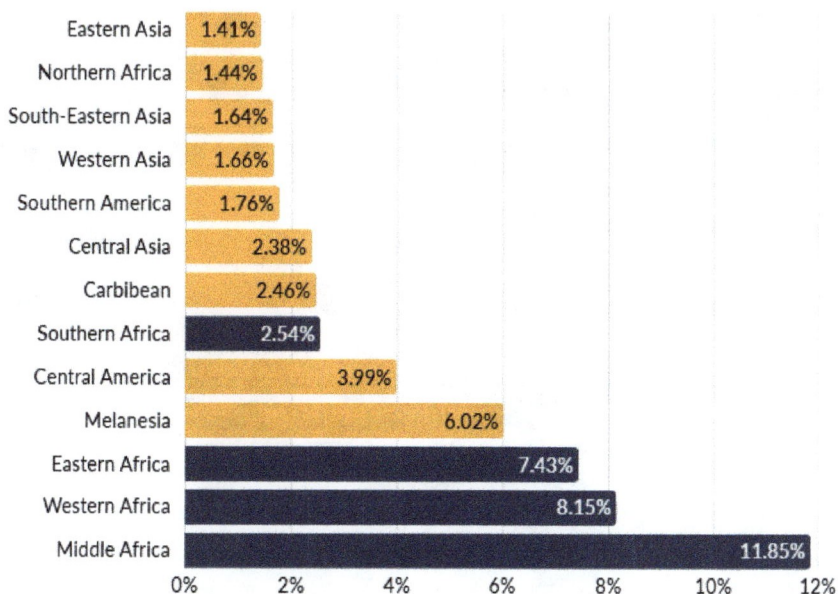

Eastern Asia	1.41%
Northern Africa	1.44%
South-Eastern Asia	1.64%
Western Asia	1.66%
Southern America	1.76%
Central Asia	2.38%
Carbibean	2.46%
Southern Africa	2.54%
Central America	3.99%
Melanesia	6.02%
Eastern Africa	7.43%
Western Africa	8.15%
Middle Africa	11.85%

Source: Alliance for Affordable Internet

The pandemic had a worsening effect on technology affordability. Research in Kenya identified that many women were forced to sell their phones during the pandemic, while others downgraded to feature phones.[25]

Financial and digital capability. In an increasingly digitized world, the ability to use technology safely and in one's own interest is critical. Closely linked to this is the ability to make financial decisions in a way that does not compromise your identity or make yourself susceptible to fraud, otherwise known as financial literacy.[26] Data from GSMA shows that there is a consistent difference across countries between men and women's confidence in using the internet on their own.

---

[25] Ibid.
[26] World Bank, *Building a Financial Education Approach* (World Bank, 2021).

In countries like DRC, India, Indonesia, and Nigeria, over 70 percent of women state they need help using the internet, much higher than men in these same countries.[27]

S&P financial literacy survey shows that only 33 percent of adults are considered financially literate. At the global level, more men (35 percent) are considered financially literate than women (30 percent). Even in developed countries, like Canada, there is a gender gap in financial literacy, estimated at 17 percentage points. In developing countries, the gap can be as large as 21 percentage points in Azerbaijan, or in the 10-percentage point range in places like Bangladesh, Yemen, or Angola.[28]

On both financial and digital capabilities, the gap between men and women begins early in life with the kinds of choices that are made by parents for their daughters versus their sons. There are often gendered expectations about roles and responsibilities that start in childhood, with a greater focus on boys to do well in school and more responsibilities for girls to help with household chores. Over time, these gendered expectations result in differences in school performance. Research shows that when girls are expected to perform worse in math, they expect less of themselves and perform worse in school.[29] These formative expectations evolve to influence women's life choices including their pursuit of employment or entrepreneurship, which in turn influences the value they place on tools such as the internet and digital technologies.

Safety and security. Women may choose to remain offline because of fear for their safety and security. GSMA reports that safety and security are the third most significant constraint to increasing women's usage of mobile phones.[30] In some cases, these fears are related to being contacted by strangers, or it may be about data security.

---

[27] GSMA, Accelerating *Digital Literacy: Empowering women to use the mobile internet* (GSMA, 2015).
[28] Chalwe-Mulinga, et al., *Break the Bias: Evidence Shows Digital Finance Risks Hit Women Hardest* (CGAP, March 2022).
[29] Hill, Catherine, et al., *Why So Few? Women in Science, Technology, Engineering, and Mathematics* (AAUW, February 2010).
[30] GSMA

A study in Jordan, India and Kenya found women were more likely to receive harassment calls than men, 58 percent as compared to only 23 percent for men. Typically, in a transaction with an agent, customers must share their phone number which could compromise their privacy.

When women get calls from strangers, this can trigger jealousy and distrust within the family, and sometimes husbands suspect women of having affairs.[31]

One mitigation strategy on safety relates to the gender of the mobile phone agent that helps customers. Typically, more women seek help from agents to conduct transactions than men. Research shows that women often prefer to use female agents. On average, women use female agents at higher rates than male agents (7.5 percentage points more likely).[32]

Beyond the gender of the agent, the regulations in place in a country also influence women's usage. IMF research finds a correlation between regulations that are protective against harassment with changes in women's access to financial and mobile services. The strength of the correlation is particularly high in Sub-Saharan Africa.[33]

Time poverty and care responsibilities. Expectations regarding roles in the household remain throughout life and result in women taking on greater unpaid care work and household chores. This often translates into women having less time to invest in business, formal employment, or leisure. At an early age, girls spend 50 percent more time doing chores than boys their same age.[34] Later in life, this phenomenon leads to women spending between 2 and 3.4 times as many hours a day as men on unpaid household chores.[35]

---

[31] Lindsey, Dominica, *Security and harassment on mobile phones: A growing concern for women in emerging markets* (GSMA Blog, November 2016).
[32] Reitzug, Fabian, Richard Chamboko, Xavier Gine and Bob Cull, *Does agent gender matter for women's financial inclusion?* (World Bank Blog, November 2020).
[33] Lagarde, Christine and Corinne Deléchat, and Monique Newiak, *Ending Harassment Helps the Economy Too* (IMF, March 2018).
[34] Hyde, Elizabeth, et al., *Time poverty: Obstacle to women's human rights, health and sustainable development* (Journal of Global Health, November 2020).
[35] Ibid

Despite progress in many European countries, this difference in how men and women spend their time, what is often termed 'time poverty' for women, exists everywhere. In Scandinavian countries, the time difference is lowest, at approximately 45 minutes more per day that women spend on unpaid work as compared to men.

Time poverty widens considerably in a place like India, where women spend five hours more on household responsibilities than men.[36] Beyond limiting income-earning opportunities, time poverty also reinforces social expectations and reinforces biases and discrimination around women's choices and participation in the economy.

The issue of time poverty translates into the perception that women do not need mobile phones or the internet because they are busy taking care of the household. The fact that many women are unable to work or become entrepreneurs because of this time poverty also reinforces the perception that they don't need these tools to engage in the digital economy.

Self-control and efficacy. The ability to control one's own time can be hampered by the social obligations to take care of others. In this way, the concept of time poverty is very related to the concepts of self-control and efficacy. Women's choices are narrowed considerably, given social obligations, to participate economically or partake in leisure activities. As such, women often feel they have low self-control as they have limited control over their own time. Similarly, they are unable to carve out the time to pursue their own goals, which reduces their sense of self-efficacy. In many societies, expectations around women's goals revolve around marriage, child rearing, caregiving, and other household responsibilities. These social norms are often internalized and reflected back by women as their own goals, with limited consideration or confidence to pursue other interests.[37]

---

[36] Salyer, Kristine, *Melinda Gates offers a solution to time poverty* (Time, February 2016).
[37] World Bank, *Measuring Women's Sense of Control and Efficacy* (World Bank, August 2021).

And, even when women are able to overcome these societal expectations and have personal goals, they are judged harshly for doing so. These expectations are evident in all countries, whether developed or developing. My own mother, who pursued her PhD in the 1970's was ostracized by my father's family for being selfish and "ruining" my father's life. A German colleague of mine who wanted to work after having her first child was judged harshly by her compatriots as a bad mother. And the list goes on. It takes enormous work on oneself to overcome such harsh societal pressures, something that few women are able to do without a strong network and support system.

Box 1: Where you live matters

Research by CFI covering Soa Palo (Brazil), Addis Ababa (Ethiopia), Delhi (India), Lagos (Nigeria) and Jakarta (Indonesia) reveals that digital adoption is impacted by where one lives. The infrastructure that is available in different markets is a major contributor or potential obstacle to uptake and usage. In this CFI research, micro and small enterprises (MSEs) in Sao Paulo were well ahead of entrepreneurs in other cities in using digital tools. Addis Ababa, on the other hand, has much more limited internet access and mobile coverage, and in turn MSEs there were far less likely to take up digital transactions. Users in India, Lagos and Jakarta were actively using social messaging apps for their businesses and social media for their marketing. Platforms like Instagram, Facebook, and TikTok helped entrepreneurs promote their businesses. Some even worked with influencers using product placements.[38]

While MSEs in all markets noted various challenges in using technology (see figure 5), there were clear benefits to firms that adopted technology solutions, particularly digital payments. Benefits included greater labor productivity, increased business growth, and improved financial resilience.

---

[38] Totolo, E., & others. *Small firms, big impact.* Center for Financial Inclusion (CFI, April, 2025).

Figure 5: Challenges with digital technology adoption

MSEs using digital solutions (%)

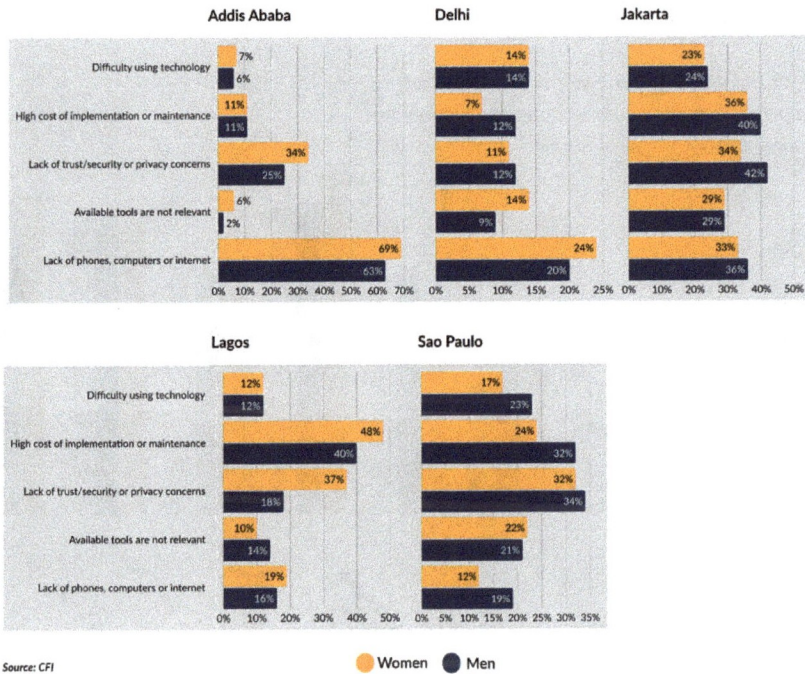

Source: CFI

● Women ● Men

The pandemic has aggravated the digital gender divide

Restrictions on in-person gatherings and cash transactions were a driving force behind the uptake of the digital economy. Despite this, women did not benefit in the same way men did. In fact, the pandemic had very real negative consequences for women, most notably the decline of their formal employment. This was initially driven by care responsibilities, whether it was to help their children with learning as schools shut down or to take care of elderly and sick relatives. Even though the pandemic restrictions are long over, women have not returned to the workforce as would have been expected. During the pandemic (2019-2020), the ILO reported a higher drop- out rate for women, compared to men. (A reported 4.2 percent in women's employment compared to 3 percent for men.[39]) But the picture varies greatly by country. In India, women's

---

[39] ILO, *Building Forward Fairer: Women's rights to work and at work at the core of the COVID-19 recovery* (ILO, July 2021).

workforce participation dropped markedly. It went from 26 percent in 2010 to just 9 percent in 2022.[40] The gap in employment between women and men in India is a shocking 58 percentage points.[41]

Figure 6: Global female work participation

As a percentage of female working age population

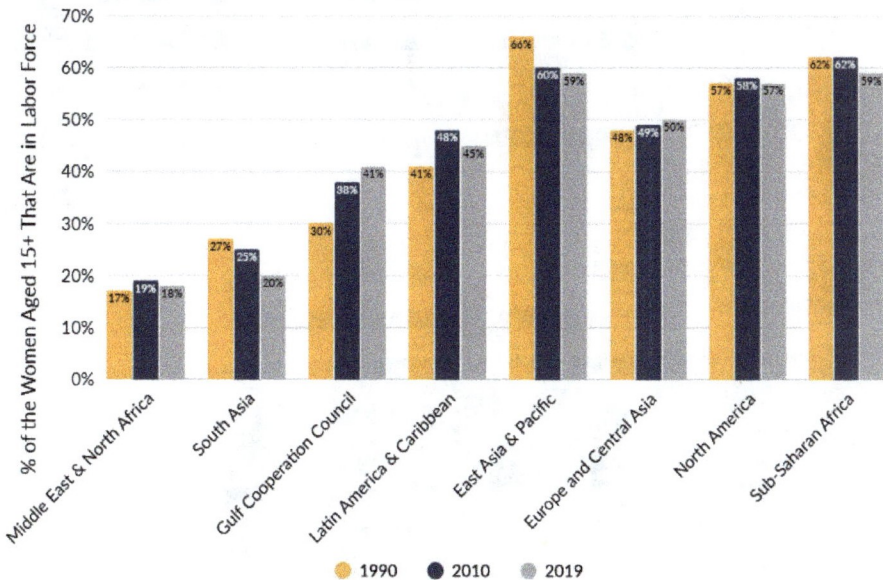

Source: World Bank

Despite the low workforce participation rate in India and South Asia more generally, women in the Middle East and North Africa (MENA) fare even worse. Data from the World Bank shows that women's workforce participation in the MENA region has declined since 2010. While there have been steady increases in women's participation in the workforce in the Gulf countries (Qatar, UAE, Saudi Arabia and Kuwait), Egypt, which is the largest country in the region, has seen a drop in women's employment and this trend has continued through 2024.[42]

---

[40] Mazumdar, Ronojoy and Chaudhary, Archana, *90% of Women in India Are Shut Out of the Workforce* (Bloomberg, June 2022).
[41] ibid
[42] PWC, *MENA Women in Work* (PWC, 2022).

Egypt's labor force participation for women has continued to deteriorate and fell as low as 18 percent in 2024.[43] This is likely a result of fewer public sector jobs, which used to be the socially acceptable forms of employment for women.

Figure 7: MENA labor force participation as a percentage of working age women

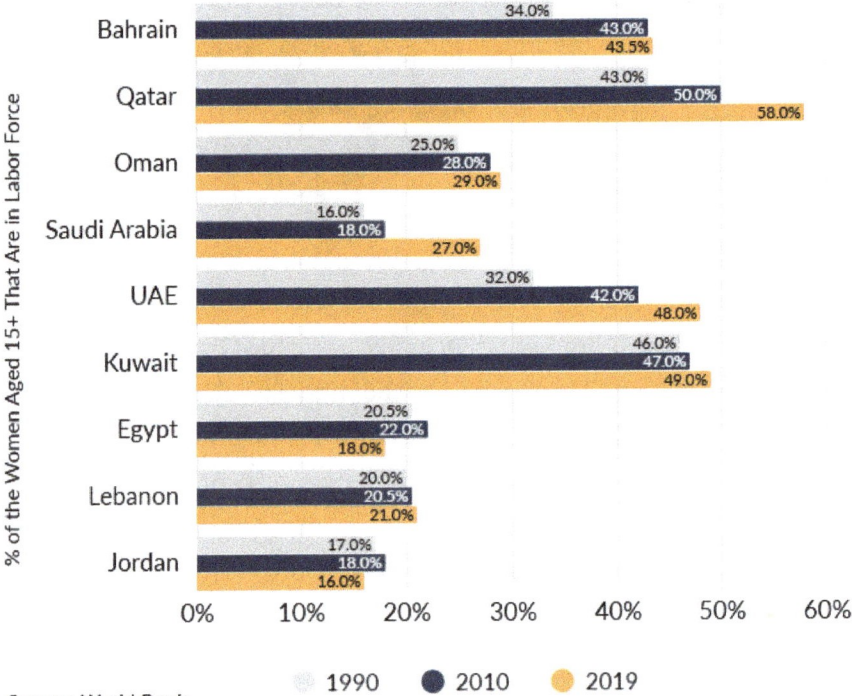

Source: *World Bank*

Promising solutions for decreasing the gender divide

Despite the many challenges women face, there are important efforts that are helping to address the digital divide.

Phone ownership. One interesting social enterprise that was built to directly address the barriers women face in accessing technology is KEIPhone.

---

[43] Arab Finance, *Top Female Labor Force Participation in Arab World in 2023* (Arab Finance, July 31, 2024).

The company operates primarily in rural East Africa and offers free smartphones to unconnected women.[44] It covers the costs of the phone by using an advertising-based revenue model. Advertisements appear on the lock screens of smartphones, and women can unlock credit for the price of data by engaging with the ad. The ads are mostly focused on content relevant to their lives, such as mobile money services, agricultural and clean energy products. The phones come with pre-installed apps that help women save, access credit, and set financial goals.[45]

Addressing gender norms and engaging men. GSMA collaborated with Telenor in India on the Sampark project to address social norms around phone ownership. The initiative targeted a key barrier to women's access to owning a phone.

The project introduced a "comboSIM" package, where purchasing a SIM for the male head of household included a free SIM for his wife. During a promotional period, topping up the primary phone automatically credited the second phone, with both SIMs benefiting from free calls between them. This approach encouraged men to provide phones for their wives and demonstrated the advantages of easier family communication. To support the initiative, GSMA and Telenor trained sales agents and launched an awareness and digital literacy campaign. After the subsidy period ended, the project found that men allowed their wives to keep their phones and continued to cover the costs of their usage.[46]

In East Africa, edutainment has been widely used to address norms around women opening their own bank accounts or engaging with men.

[44] M'bale, Amani and Graham Wright, *Can Access to Smartphones Bridge the Digital Divide in Sub-Saharan Africa?* (NextBillion November 2022).
[45] Wason, Wes, *Free Fintech-Enabled Smartphones Coming to Unbanked Women in Africa from DreamStart Labs and KEIPhone*, (PR Newswire May 2022).
[46] Burjorjee, D., El-Zoghbi, M., & others, *Social norms change for women's financial inclusion* (CGAP, July 2017).

A series called Makutano Junction[47] created by the media firm Mediae, addresses many of the difficult topics that men and women must address in their real lives and provides a way for women to discuss these issues and gain confidence in making change. The series has had a measurable impact on behavior. For women watching the show, 138,000 opened bank accounts compared to no change for non-viewers. Those viewing the show also reported acquiring financial skills. Banks also observed changes in engagement after the show, with viewers more actively using ATMs and mobile money.[48]

Awareness and digital literacy. Women in many low- and middle-income countries engage with and participate in various types of collectives. These can be called self-help groups (SHGs), savings groups, or SACCOs. These groups often serve as support networks and also a major source of information, in addition to their core mandate, whether that's savings, credit or both. According to NABARD,[49] India has more than 85 million women involved in women's collectives, or what amounts to 8 million groups.[50] Internet Saathi, launched in 2015 as a partnership between Google India, Intel, and Tata Trusts, sought to close the digital gender divide in rural India. The program empowered local women, called "Saathis," by training them as digital educators within their communities. To effectively reach and educate women in these communities, the program leverages existing networks of SHGs and women's federations. These Saathis teach SHG members how to use the internet, smartphones, and digital services, fostering greater digital inclusion. The training sessions are often conducted in locations accessible to SHG members, such as community centers, schools, or SHG meeting places.

---

[47] See video at:
https://www.youtube.com/watch?v=9EYixvLj5UI&list=PLQzxCCV93lUHvzu28CnJ6GRzHDYuqDk_u
[48] Women's World Banking, *How a popular TV show shifted social norms around women's banking habits in Kenya* (WWB, June 2017).
[49] National Bank for Agriculture and Rural Development
[50] Buteau, S., Sreenivasan, V., Narasimhan, M., & Kumar, J. V. A., *From margins to mainstream: State and private initiatives shaping women's collectives in the digital economy* (LEAD at Krea University, June 2023).

This approach ensures that the training is integrated into the existing social structures of the community, facilitating greater participation and impact. By 2021, the initiative had impacted over 30 million women across 300,000 villages, significantly advancing digital literacy among rural women.[51]

Seeing such promising innovation and concrete results shows that the barriers women face to access and participate in the digital economy are not insurmountable. It takes a combination of knowledge, creativity, and commitment. Scaling these types of solutions will require support by government, the development community, and the private sector. The latter half of the book discusses the stakeholders and their roles.

---

[51] Business Standard, *15M women across 150,000 villages benefit from the Internet Saathi program* (Business Standard, May 2018).

Chapter 3
Gateway to the Digital Economy: Digital Finance

"Digital financial inclusion" can be defined broadly as digital access to, and use of, formal financial services by excluded and underserved populations. Such services should be suited to customers' needs, and delivered responsibly, at a cost affordable to customers and sustainable for providers. There are three key components of any such digital financial services: a digital transactional platform, retail agents, and the use by customers and agents of a device, most commonly a mobile phone – to transact via the platform."
Tim Lyman and Kate Lauer, CGAP

Every industry has been affected by the digital economy. Hollywood movies are challenged by streaming services. Newspapers are challenged by social media and influencers who drive the news narrative. The financial services industry is in the midst of transformation, both from within as financial services players themselves take on digital tools and channels to adapt to the new age and from without, where technology companies, FinTechs and non-finance companies (like ride hailing or e-commerce) embedding finance into their operations are chipping away at customers who are either unhappy or were never served in the first place by the traditional financial system. Where banks were the entry point into the financial system, today the gateway is any payment, whether it's using an app or swiping a QR code.

The data that is produced by these seemingly innocuous transactions are paving the way for more complex products such as credit and insurance.[52]

The promise that technology can transform finance is enormous. It can reduce transaction costs. It can completely sidestep physical infrastructure. It can make people without credit histories or collateral become credit-worthy by using their transaction data. In a nutshell, its promise is about making the financial system more inclusive. And an inclusive financial system is what opens up broader participation in the economy. The ride-hailing apps work primarily because they allow the rider to pay electronically, and the company can see those transactions, take their share, and pay the driver their share. Or at least that's the promise.

More people are included in the financial system than ever before

Data from the World Bank Findex tells us that technology is indeed expanding access. During the period 2011 to 2024, account access for adults increased by more than 50 percent globally, now reaching 79 percent of adults. And the gender gap between men and women, which had been stuck at nine percentage points for nearly a decade finally dropped to five percentage points in 2025 in low- and middle-income countries. With countries like India, the gap in account ownership has been completely eliminated.[53]

Undeniably, the COVID pandemic had a massive push for digital adoption. As governments-imposed restrictions on in-person interactions while simultaneously launching the largest social transfer schemes to help individuals and firms survive the pandemic, more and more people in developing countries opened digital wallets and bank accounts in order to transact and receive government payments.

---

[52] Economist, *As payment systems go digital they are changing global finance* (Economist Special Report, May 15, 2025).
[53] Findex 2024

According to the latest Findex, approximately 61 percent of adults globally made or received a digital payment. This includes using a card, phone or the internet. [54]

What's driving digital finance around the world?

There are now more than 1.7 billion registered mobile money accounts globally, according to GSMA's latest State of the Industry Report.[55] While the rate of growth has slowed somewhat, it is still a respectable 12 percent growth rate from 2021. Mobile money has been a major driver of formal financial service access and usage, particularly in Sub-Saharan Africa. The story is somewhat different in other regions of the world. E-commerce companies and ride-hailing – collectively known as platforms- are driving usage in Asia. In Western nations, where banks and credit cards are already quite dominant, BigTechs and FinTechs are the main drivers of new solutions.

Figure 1: Actors driving inclusive digital finance in different regions of the world

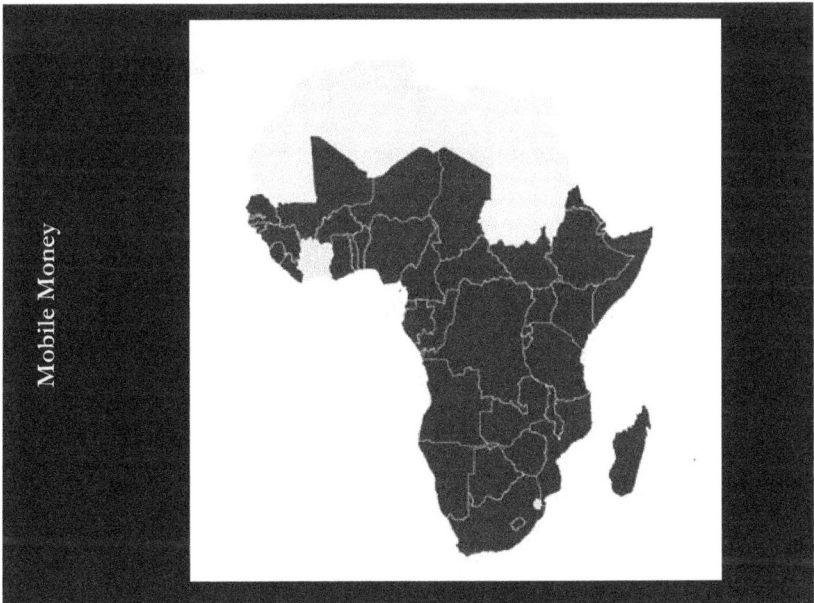

[54] Ibid
[55] GSMA, *The State of the Industry Report on Mobile Money* (GSMA, 2024).

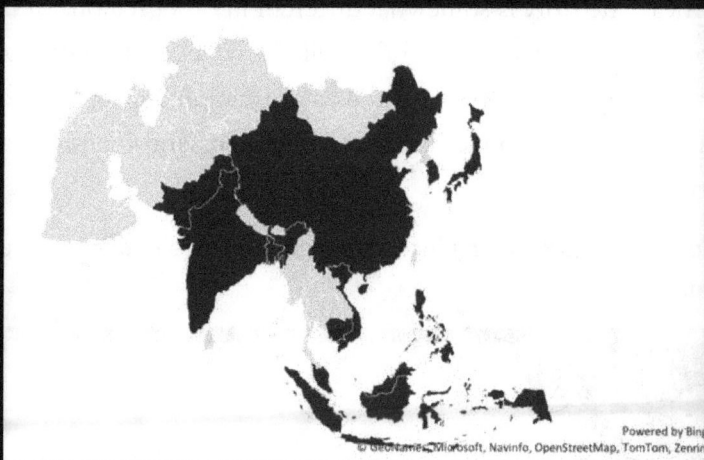

Figure 2 below shows the extent of mobile money service in SSA as compared to other regions of the world. In fact, SSA accounts for half of the entire global mobile money deployment. SSA also has the largest number of accounts, at 835 million. It is a region where not only does the number of services proliferate, but also the volume of transactions is the highest in the world at US$912 billion.

The rise of mobile money in SSA is attributed to several key important differentiators:

- An enabling regulatory framework where regulators allowed mobile network operators to offer wallets without banking licenses. This compared to other regions where typically banks controlled all financial services.

- Large unbanked populations also had access to mobile phones. This latent demand meant that customers were ready to meet their needs through new channels.

- Fierce competition among mobile network operators that were looking for ways to differentiate themselves and create stickiness with their customers. Offering mobile money allowed them to address other pain points their customers faced.

Figure 2: Regional growth of mobile money 2024 (and growth since 2023)

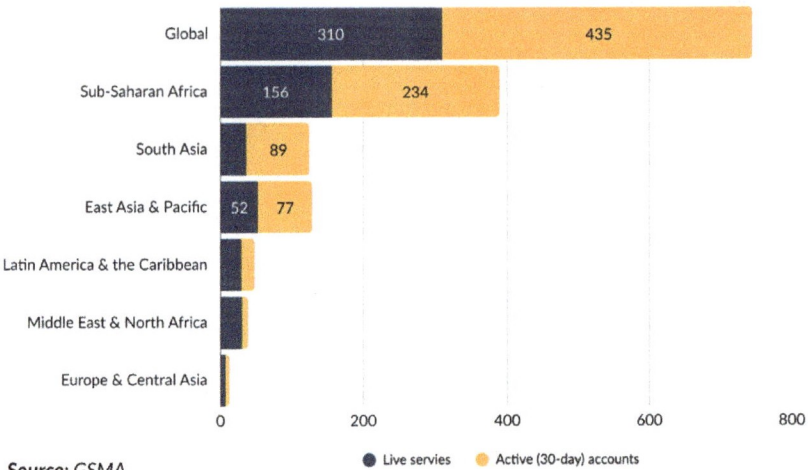

Source: GSMA

Embedded finance - every firm is now a finance firm

While in SSA mobile money has led the way to digital finance and the digital economy, in East Asia and the Pacific, platform companies have been the biggest driver of uptake. Platforms include e-commerce, ride-hailing, and other digital services that bring demand and supply together.

Nowhere has this been more pronounced than in China, where companies like Alibaba, which owns Ant Group, is one of the largest payments and financial services companies in the world, considered to be the 6th largest. Ant Group serves over 1.6 billion buyers and 90 million merchants.[56] Ant Group is not only focused on payments, but also offers credit, investment, insurance, foreign exchange, and international transfers.

Across Asia, e-commerce is driving the usage of digital financial services. After China, both India and Indonesia have robust e-commerce markets. In Indonesia, one of the most successful e-commerce platforms is Bukalapak. It started in 2010 as an online marketplace for small enterprises, helping them source, supply and access customers. The company now serves over 100 million customers and 7 million merchants. It's evolved and is now a super app offering financial services, logistics support, business-to-business services, and support for both online and offline retailers.[57]

In India, companies like FlipKart dominate in e-commerce with 100 million users and 80,000 merchants; PayTM in financial services with 300 million users and 21 million merchants;[58] and Ola in ride-hailing, accounting for around 65 percent of the market share of the ride-hailing business in India.[59]

BigTechs and FinTechs

In Europe and North America, where most consumers already have bank accounts and credit cards, the allure of mobile money has not been as compelling. Instead, banks offer digital banking apps and the BigTech players, such as Google and Apple, offer digital wallets where consumers can store their credit card data or link to their bank accounts.

---

[56] Asian Banking & Finance, *Ant Int'l sees growth in 4 divisions, Alipay+ holds 1.6 billion users* (Asian Banking & Finance, January 2025).
[57] Mulia, Kamila, *The 9-year journey of Bukalapak: Growing beyond e-commerce* (KrEurope, January 2019).
[58] Digital Vidya, *Top Startups In India 2025: Business Model Explained* (Digital Vidya, *December 2024).*
[59] Product Monk, *How did Ola become this big?* (Product Monk, August 2024).

FinTechs have emerged where there are pain points in the current financial systems, mostly linked to transfers between people, services for small merchants, international transfers and retail investing.

PayPal, Venmo and a host of other such FinTechs enable friends to split the bill or people to pay small merchants quickly without waiting days for a payment to clear through the financial system.

Sending money internationally has been another pain point where international transfers can take a week and can be quite costly. Sending $200 internationally can cost a U.S.-based customer $12.80, or approximately 6.4 percent.[60] Companies such as Remitly and Xoom (owned by PayPal), offer much faster and cheaper options. Remitly, for example, charges only $1.99 for transfers from the U.S. to Mexico and $3.99 for transfers to India. For large transfers over $1,000, it even waives the fees.[61]

Supporting small merchants with digital payments is another vibrant space where FinTech and BigTech innovations have proliferated in the U.S. and Europe. In the U.S., companies such as Stripe and Square offer tailored solutions for small merchants. Square offers point of sale hardware and software and also supports small merchants with bill payments, payroll and access to credit. Square also works in Europe through Square International.

Mollie, a Dutch FinTech, supports local EU payment methods such as iDEAL, SEPA, or PayPal, and allows simple integration without complicated setup. It has limited onboarding and doesn't lock customers into the service.[62]

---

[60] Migration Data Portal
[61] Remitly.com
[62] The European Payments Experts, *8 best stripe alternatives for European businesses.*

Connecting low-value retail investors is another area where FinTechs have played a big role in Europe and North America. Perhaps no other FinTech has received as much attention as Robinhood.[63] It offers free trading for U.S. equities, ETFs, options (no per-contract fees), and crypto assets. It also offers fractional shares allowing investors to own as little as $1 in a company. While Robinhood has been controversial with several outages in 2020 linked to excessive trading of meme stocks like GameStop and its inability to meet clearinghouse collateral requirements, it continues to flourish in the U.S., especially among young and previously unbanked consumers.

Payments are the gateway product

Whether it's the convenience of shopping online or tapping your card or phone at the local bodega, the path to using digital finance is typically a payment transaction. Figure 3 below depicts the massive rise in payment usage in different regions of the world. OECD countries are clearly well ahead of the rest of the world, but Eastern Europe, and East Asia and the Pacic regions are showing remarkable growth in the use of digital payments. Latin America and SSA are not too far behind.

---

[63] Bankrate, *Robinhood review 2025* (Bankrate, June 2025).

Figure 3: Usage digital payments at least once a year

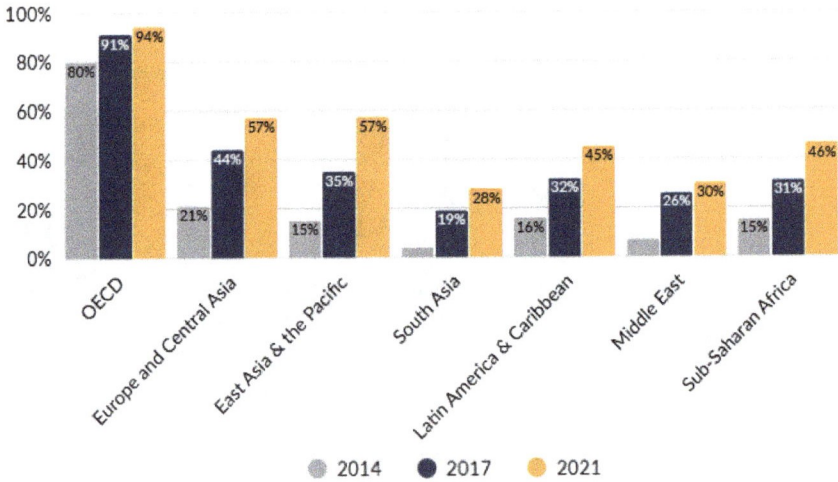

Bar chart showing usage of digital payments at least once a year by region for 2014, 2017, and 2021:

Region	2014	2017	2021
OECD	80%	91%	94%
Europe and Central Asia	21%	44%	57%
East Asia & the Pacific	15%	35%	57%
South Asia		19%	28%
Latin America & Caribbean	16%	32%	45%
Middle East		26%	30%
Sub-Saharan Africa	15%	31%	46%

Legend: 2014, 2017, 2021

Source: World Bank

Typically, digital payments usage is accelerated by important investments in fast payment systems. This is a trend around the world, best depicted by PIX in Brazil. Usage of PIX has been astronomical as seen in Figure 4. In just three years usage has gone from 18 percent of the population to 63 percent of the population. PIX is a secure instant payment system that's available 24 hours a day and is free for individuals and only costs 0.33 percent for merchants. This lower price point is significant compared to 1.13 percent for debit cards and 2.34 percent for credit cards.[64]

---

[64] IMF, *Pix: Brazil's Successful Instant Payment System* (IMF, July 2023).

Figure 4: Usage of PIX in Brazil between Nov 2020-Dec 2023

Millions, % change and % of population

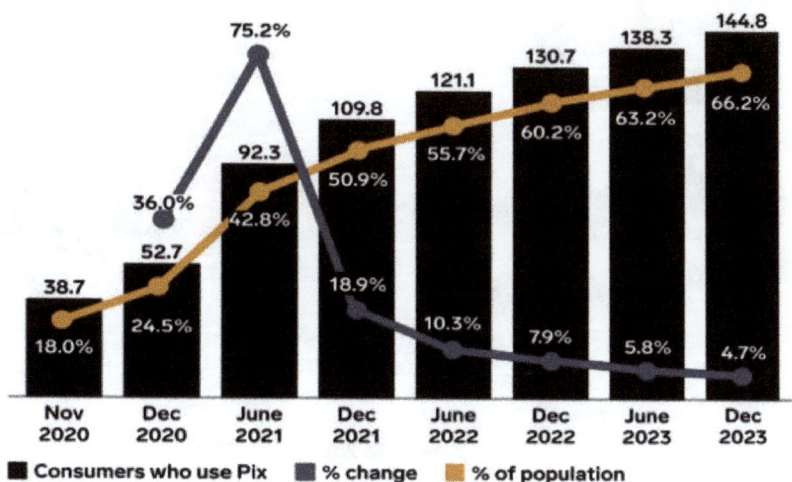

Consumers who use Pix ■ % change ■ % of population

Source: IMF

Once a laggard, Egypt is a country that is replicating global trends in digital payments. In April 2022, the Central Bank authorized InstaPay which now has over 12.5 million registered users and a volume of 2.9 trillion Egyptian pounds (more than $57 billion) by the end of 2024.[65]

Cash is still essential

Despite the marked increase in digital finance around the world, the use of cash is not yet dead and it's unlikely to ever be. Research by CGAP on cash-in, cash-out (CICO) agents align closely with the uptake of digital payments (See Figure 5).[66] The more agents there are to load wallets with cash and to take out cash to use for school payments, utility bills or give to your children, the more likely people are to use digital finance.

---

[65] Central Bank of Egypt, *Central Bank of Egypt Issues New Decrees for Extending the Exemption of Individuals from Transfer Fees via Instant Payment Network and InstaPay Application for a Renewable Period of 3 Months* (Central Bank of Egypt, December 2024).

[66] Hernandez, Emilio and Blackburn, Christopher, *Agent Networks at the Last Mile* (CGAP, September 2020).

A major reason for this correlation is the fact that in many developing countries, digital literacy is still limited among certain groups. Many low-income people are also in informal work where payment is still in cash. Imagine a house cleaner or a market vendor in a rural community; it's likely they are still operating in cash. Even in developed markets like the U.S., the use of cash has remained stable and digital payments are disrupting checks rather than cash.[67]   Furthermore, for small and informal businesses, cash remains the best way to avoid taxation and scrutiny by tax authorities.

Figure 5: Mobile money use increases with the availability of CICO agents in 9 markets

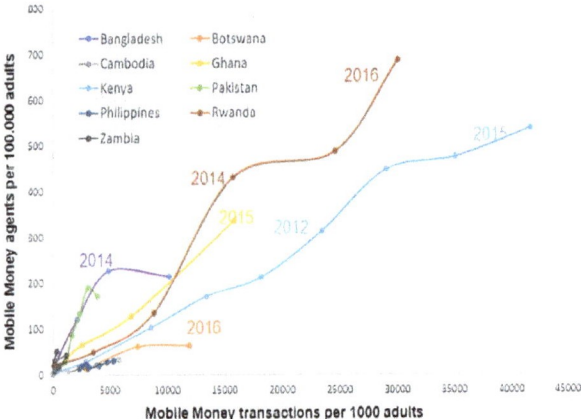

Source: Proximity Matters, Five Case Studies in Closing the CICO Gap, CGAP, 2018

Governments have been important enablers

Digital finance has taken off in countries where governments have played an important enabling role. India is probably the most well-known case of the government taking a proactive vision and investing in digital public infrastructure that has laid the groundwork for private sector innovation.

---

[67] CGAP, *Cash Is King in Merchant Payments* (CGAP, October 2019).

Central Banks have been keen to test and learn from new innovations using regulatory sandboxes. The concept emerged in the UK in 2016, when the Financial Conduct Authority (FCA), encouraged financial services providers to test their products live with consumers but in a confined and safe space. All types of providers were encouraged, whether regulated or unregulated and included FinTechs, big banks (e.g., Barclays, HSBC, Nationwide), and BigTech companies.[68] By 2020, CGAP identified 16 regulatory sandboxes around the world, hosting 134 companies. As of 2025, the IMF reports over 95 regulatory sandboxes, while other sources estimate even higher numbers.[69]

Risks are also rising

Despite this tremendous transformation that is happening in the financial sector, which is expanding access to new users in every corner of the world, the risks are also proliferating. In some markets, the growth has been so phenomenal and out of step with the government's ability to supervise, eliciting some governments to step in to slow down progress. Most notable was the Chinese government's decision to halt the planned flotation of Ant Group in November 2020.[70] Meta's foray into finance[71] through the launch of its online currency, Libra and later called Diem, was also halted.[72]

In low and middle-income countries, the risks to consumers continue to escalate and regulators and supervisors have been less aggressive in stepping in. Risks for low-income users come from many directions, whether it's the technology itself, the agents they need, or the lack of recourse given the number of players who are now in the value chain of every transaction.

---

[68] Jenik, Ivo and Lauer, Kate, *Regulatory Sandboxes and Financial Inclusion* (CGAP, October 2017).

[69] Bains, Parma and Wu, Caroline, *Institutional Arrangements for Fintech Regulation: Supervisory Monitoring* (IMF, 2023).

[70] The Banker, *Ant's IPO halt marks shift for China's fintech scene* (The Banker, January 2021).

[71] Previously Facebook

[72] Nijland, Shikko and Lycklama, *Douwe, Why trust and timing were key libras downfall* (INNOPAY, August 2022).

CGAP's research on mobile money points to several worrying trends since 2015; the rise of fraud, data misuse, and inadequate redress. Also of concern is the lack of transparency by many of the providers in the digital finance space.[73]

One of the most striking concerns is the rise in fraud since the pandemic. A study by researchers in Switzerland tracking apps in 71 countries found that "most downloaded mobile apps in a number of countries following the outbreak of COVID-19 include finance-related apps that show signs of being either predatory or entirely fraudulent." The apps were shadowing government cash transfer programs as a result of the pandemic, aiming to get people's private data.[74]

Another growing concern is over-indebtedness: with digital credit, borrowing is now as easy as a click. In 2016, the Center for Effective Global Action (CEGA) at the University of California, Berkeley created the Digital Credit Observatory with funding from the Gates Foundation to better understanding the effects of digital credit on low and middle-income countries. Research by CEGA affiliates in Malawi finds that consumers using digital credit are not fully aware of the loan terms or conditions and thus often pay late without realizing the substantial implications financially and on their credit histories.

Over 47 percent of borrowers repay their loans fully but do so late, and in turn incur effective interest rates of 27 percent as compared to the 10 percent had they paid on time.[75]

---

[73] Mulenga, Marjorie, Duflos, Eric and Coetze, Gerhard, *The Evolution of the Nature and Scale of DFS Consumer Risks: A Review of Evidence* (CGAP, February 2022).
[74] Fu, Jonathan and Mishra, Mrinal, *Combating the Rise in Fraudulent Fintech Apps* (CFI, December 21, 2020).
[75] Dupas, Pascaline, et al., *The impact of digital credit in low-income countries* (VOXEU, March 8, 2022).

Other researchers exploring digital credit markets in Côte d'Ivoire, Ghana, India, Kenya and Tanzania, find that consumers in Ghana and Kenya are highly likely to take up digital credit (80 percent and 54 percent respectively) and that there is a greater likelihood of financial delinquency when these borrowers take up digital loans than those who take traditional loans from a financial institution.[76]

Sometimes, customers are borrowing without even knowing it. For example, there is massive growth in buy-now, pay-later (BNPL) payment options which most individuals do not realize are credit. In the U.S., there is rapid uptake of BNPL payment options and this has led to an increase in overall spending. Researchers looked at transaction data before the introduction of BNPL and after and found that purchasing decisions went from 17 percent to 26 percent after BNPL was introduced.[77]

Using technology to monitor and address risks

Increasingly, regulators and supervisors are waking up to the emerging risks and are investing in how technology can help them keep up with the scammers and fraudsters. One of the most important investments supervisors are making is improving market monitoring and recourse systems, which help them track the kinds of risks that are happening in the market while also enabling them to get the data they need to course correct.

The Bank of England, always at the forefront of innovation, has been collaborating with the BIS Innovation Hub's London Centre in a project called Project Hertha. The initiative is a pilot using AI to detect suspicious behavior and illicit networks in real-time payment flows. Monitoring these transactions, the initiative was able to increase illicit

---

[76] Storchi, Gianluca, *Does digital credit lead to over-indebtedness? Evidence from a study* (GSMA, February 24, 2025).
[77] Ang, Dionysius and Maesen, Stijn, *How "Buy Now, Pay Later" Is Changing Consumer Spending* (Harvard Business Review, November 26, 2024).

account detection by 12 percent and improve the identification of new financial crime patterns compared to traditional methods by 26 percent.[78]

In developing countries, one of the most successful initiatives to monitor market conduct has been undertaken by the Philippines Central Bank, which developed a chatbot called BOB, which stands for BSP (Bank Sentral NG Pilipinas) Online Buddy. Consumers can submit their complaints through various channels including BSP Facebook, the BSP mobile app, or BSP webchat. Traditional channels, like submitting a form via email or online, are also feasible. By collecting real-time complaints, the Central Bank can identify concentrations of risk and then focus its supervisory efforts on those actors with the highest numbers of complaints. The use of BOB has greatly increased efficiency of handling consumer complaints. In 2020, BOB handled only 15 percent of cases, but this surged to 58 percent by the second quarter of 2021;[79] by 2024, BOB was handling 95 percent of consumer complaints.[80] The rapidity of the complaint processing has resulted in increased consumer trust and adoption. Furthermore, 69 percent of users are satisfied with the process.[81]

The Central Bank of the Philippines is also prioritizing efforts to improve consumer awareness of fraud and scams. Box 1 below is an example of the type of information that the Central Bank is issuing to consumers to help them stay ahead of the scammers.

---

[78] Lacovcich, Silvia, *Bank of England trials AI to detect fraud in real-time payments* (FSTech, June 2025).
[79] Philippines Information Agency (PIA), *More financial consumers tapping BSP's chatbot* (PIA, July 23, 2021).
[80] Reyes, Maria Asumpta Estefanie C., *BSP emphasizes online assistance availability for financial consumers* (PIA, September 9, 2024).
[81] Philippines Information Agency (PIA), *More financial consumers tapping BSP's chatbot* (PIA, July 23, 2021).

Box 1: Improving consumer awareness of scams and fraud in the Philippines

Protect Yourself From Fraud and Scam

What is a Scam?

A fraudulent scheme typically committed to cheat a victim into giving money resulting in the victim's financial loss.

Protect Yourself From Fraud and Scam

How do Frauds Happen?

False Representation

Fraudsters usually pose as someone they are not. They prey on people's emotions to manipulate our human tendency to trust. They tell stories that either resonate to our sensitive side or to our desires and aspirations. Then they employ tactics to induce pressure.

Phantom Riches

Fraudsters promise the prospect of instant and guaranteed wealth. People tend to forget that "If something sounds too good to be true, it usually is a scam."

Social Consensus

To increase trust, fraudsters claim that others have already joined or contributed to a cause at hand, like an investment opportunity.

Source: BSP.gov

Academics have been monitoring social media chatter to help detect fraud and scams. Innovations for Poverty Action (IPA) analyzed social media posts (Twitter and Facebook) and online reviews (Google Play Store) to track potential scams and other abuses on FinTech apps. The research focused on three countries: Kenya, Nigeria, and Uganda. They categorized complaints into seven categories including customer care issues, operational failures, fees & charges, fraud, data privacy, lending issues and advertisements. Figure 6 below captures the main findings, with customer care the highest area of concern for users followed by operational challenges. Using social media monitoring presents an interesting and relatively low-cost method for regulators and supervisors to identify potential areas of risks. The method can help identify spikes in complaints by specific user segments or with specific institutions signaling concerns and potentially warranting heightened supervision.

Figure 6: Analysis of customer complaints in Kenya, Nigeria, and Uganda

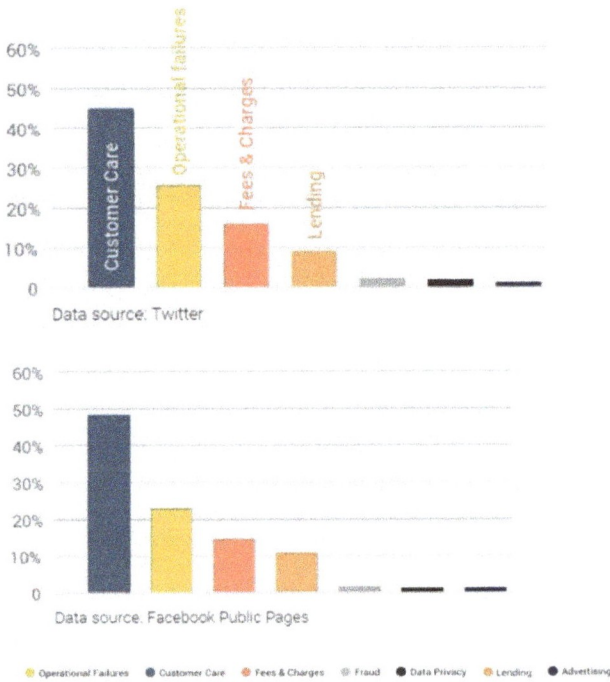

Data source: Twitter

Data source: Facebook Public Pages

● Operational Failures ● Customer Care ● Fees & Charges ● Fraud ● Data Privacy ● Lending ● Advertising

Source: IPA

Offering safer payment alternatives

Digital currencies have proliferated widely, and adoption has been surprisingly high in some developing countries, particularly those with high inflation. For example, in 2025, nearly 41 percent of adults in Nigeria either used or held cryptocurrencies. This is one of the highest rates in the world and is mostly a result of the high inflationary environment and the waning of the naira.[82]   But in other countries, like Vietnam, over 20 percent of the population held cryptocurrencies mostly for remittances or e-commerce purchases.[83]

---

[82] Financial Times, *Transcript: The ABCs of CBDCs* (Financial Times, August 2024).
[83] CoinFlexify, *The Growing World of Cryptocurrency: Global Adoption Trends in 2025* (CoinFlexify, April 2025).

Cryptocurrencies are proliferating in countries where there is limited trust in central authorities, offering users a completely decentralized and anonymous way to transact.

The risks of cryptocurrencies have been widely discussed, given the massive drop in Bitcoin prices (from $69,000 in 2021 to $17,000 in 2022)[84] and the crypto 'winter' that took place in 2022-23. The market crash of stable coins (Terra ecosystem) wiped out $45 billion in market value in just a few days.

As unregulated securities, cryptocurrencies may appear to be a great solution to hedging local currencies or facilitating international transfers, but they pose many risks, particularly for low-capacity consumers.

No country went as far as El Salvador with cryptocurrencies which officially adopted Bitcoin as legal tender in 2021. The government believed that formal adoption of Bitcoin by the state would encourage investment, remittances, and financial inclusion. However, usage of Bitcoin, despite government backing, was still limited with only 1 percent of remittances using the cryptocurrency. Trust in the currency was still not prevalent, and government backing did little to bolster this trust. Later, the IMF required El Salvador to scale back its Bitcoin experiment to access its much needed $1.4 billion assistance package.[85]

Many countries have opted to mitigate the risks of cryptocurrencies by offering their own digital currencies to serve as a safer, regulated option. According to the Atlantic Council (See Figure 7), there have been three full-scale central bank digital currency (CBDCs) launches (Nigeria, Jamaica, the Bahamas), while 44 are in pilot phase, and many others are either in development or research phases.

---

[84] Kerner, Sean Michael, *Crypto winter explained* (TechTarget, June 2023).
[85] Hernández, José Ignacio, *In El Salvador, Bitcoin's Retreat Left Valuable Lessons* (Americas Quarterly, March 17, 2025).

While CBDCs represent an alternative to cryptocurrencies, they remain in the hands of central authorities and thus are perceived as potentially risky in another way, they could enable surveillance by the state. Thus, they do not fully replace the decentralization and anonymity offered by cryptocurrencies.

Figure 7: Where central banks have issued digital currencies

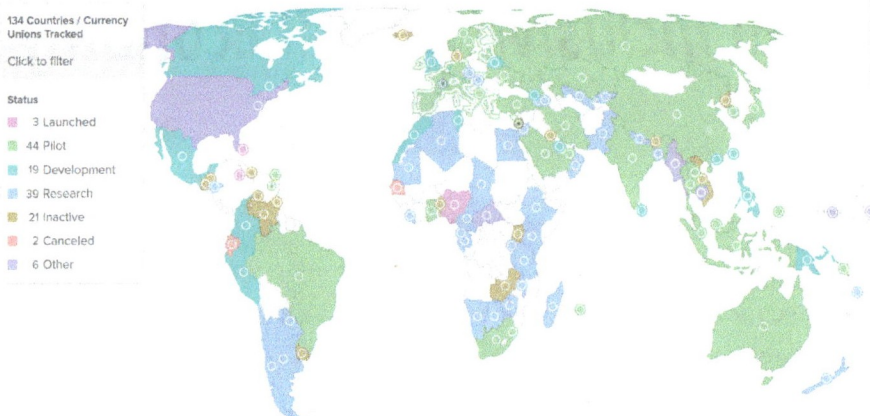

Source: Atlantic Council, CBDC Tracker

Gateway to the digital economy for many users

Digital payments have been one of the clearest pathways to connecting people to the digital economy. But ensuring that the digital financial system is accessible and safe for all types of users, particularly those with limited capacity, remains a challenge. The speed at which technology is evolving is exponential, while consumers, regulators, and supervisors may lag in their ability to keep up with these innovations. Harnessing technology to address this gap needs to be a priority if the financial system, and the digital economy at large, is one that is responsible and safe for all types of users. At the same time, we must acknowledge the barriers that exist for many users and look for alternative solutions that enable them to prosper, regardless of their digital footprint.

Chapter 4
An *Inclusive* Digital Economy

In chapter 1, we discussed what makes an economy digital. And in Chapter 2, we saw that certain segments in society, such as women or rural households, may not be fully benefiting from the digitalization of the economy. What would it take to make a digital economy inclusive so that everyone can participate fully and benefit from it?

It is an odd time to be speaking about inclusion, given the backlash that has become mainstream in 2025. The entire Diversity, Equity, and Inclusion (DEI) field has been aggressively attacked by the likes of Elon Musk and President Donald Trump. Bill Ackman is most famous for his publication in 2024 on X (formerly Twitter), which sharply condemned DEI policies. He focused especially on Harvard and called DEI initiatives inherently racist and linked them to antisemitism and discrimination against white and Asian individuals.[86] Much of the attacks on Universities in the United States today emanate from these initial attacks by Ackerman. Most recently, the Department of Justice forced the University of Virginia to remove its president—James Ryan—after he supported DEI efforts.[87]

---

[86] Tan, Kwan Wei Kevin, *Bill Ackman just posted a 4,000-word essay at 2 a.m. cataloging his arguments on why DEI needs to die* (Business Insider, January 2024).
[87] Washington Post, *The DOJ just forced out U-Va.'s president. It's time to take a stand* (June 2025).

As a result of the concerted anti-DEI movement in the United States, many companies have been quickly editing their websites and policy statements to remove trigger words like 'gender' and 'inclusion.' Target removed its DEI page on its website and replaced it with "Belonging at the Bullseye."[88] USAA eliminated DEI language from its website and instead used the language of 'belonging,' though underlying programs remain.[89] Many others like IBM, Qualcomm, Ogilvy have since dismantled their DEI departments and policies.

Despite these setbacks, the path toward inclusive societies is in no way halted. In fact, many companies have rejected the knee-jerk responses against DEI. Disney shareholders overwhelmingly voted against a proposal by the National Center for Public Policy Research to cease participation in the Human Rights Campaign's Corporate Equality Index with only ~1 percent of shareholders voting in favor of the proposal.[90] A similar proposal at Costco was also voted down by 98 percent of shareholders. JPMorgan reaffirmed its commitment to DEI, with its CEO, Jamie Dimon, noting its importance to innovation and financial profitability.[91]

In Europe, many companies have tried to appease their U.S.-based subsidiaries, but continue to reaffirm their commitment to diversity and inclusion in their European operations. In Germany, a survey of firms found that 90 percent of companies would continue their DEI work unchanged.[92]

---

[88] O'Loughlin, Henry, *103 Companies Reducing/Ending DEI: Master Rollback List* (Build Remote, July 2025).
[89] Wright, Zachary-Taylor, *USAA replaces DEI language with 'belonging' amid federal scrutiny* (My San Antonio, February 2025).
[90] Business Insider, *Disney Shareholders Reject Anti-DEI Proposal, Business Insider* (Business Insider, March 2025).
[91] Diversity.com, *Corporate DEI Under Fire: How Companies Are Responding to Trump's Executive Order* (Diversity.com, January 27, 2025).
[92] DW (Deutsche Welle), *How Trump's Anti-Woke Push Affects German Firms' DEI Policy* (DW, 2025).

Some countries in Europe, like France and Belgium, have rejected the anti-DEI efforts. The French Foreign Trade Minister, Laurent Saint-Martin, and Gender Equality Minister Aurore Bergé called efforts to undermine DEI in French firms "unacceptable" and asserted that French businesses would refuse to comply.[93] The Belgian Deputy Prime Minister Jan Jambon and Equality Minister Rob Beenders have publicly noted that Belgium has a "culture of non-discrimination" and vowed to uphold DEI under domestic law.[94] And, the European Commission has stated that DEI is central to EU values and insisted that any U.S. directive affecting EU procurement must align with WTO rules.

Developing countries have been affected more directly by the anti-DEI push of the Trump administration. The U.S. issued Executive Order 14169 (Jan 2025) halting all foreign aid programs tied to "gender or DEI ideology."[95] Some countries have sought to negotiate to seek exceptions for extremely vulnerable groups (Liberia),[96] while others have asked for alternative solutions that can help address vulnerability (Kenya).[97]

In Chapter 5, we'll delve deeper into how to address the backlash against diversity and inclusion, and in Chapter 10, we'll discuss other solutions to financing these initiatives in light of aid cuts.

---

[93] Euronews, *US Efforts to Eliminate Diversity Initiatives in Europe Face Backlash From Some Countries*, (Euronews, March 31, 2025).
[94] ibid
[95] Federal Register, *Reevaluating and Realigning United States Foreign Aid* (Federal Register, January 30, 2025).
[96] U.S. Department of State, *Emergency Humanitarian Waiver to Foreign Assistance Pause* (U.S. State Department, 2025).
[97] Kenyans.co.ke, *Foreign Affairs PS Korir Singoei Optimistic Trump Will Provide Alternatives Financial,* (Kenyans, 2025).

What is an inclusive economy

Let's start from the beginning. Since it's 2025, there's no better place to start than ChatGPT. I asked ChatGPT about the definition of an inclusive economy, and the answer I got was:

An inclusive economy is an economic system that strives to provide equal opportunities and benefits to all individuals, regardless of their background or socioeconomic status. In an inclusive economy, everyone has access to quality education, healthcare, and job opportunities, and no one is excluded or discriminated against based on their race, gender, religion, or any other characteristic.

An inclusive economy also aims to reduce income inequality and promote economic growth that benefits all members of society, not just a privileged few. This can be achieved through policies that promote fair taxation, equitable distribution of wealth, and investment in infrastructure and social programs that benefit everyone.

In summary, an inclusive economy is one that creates a level playing field for all individuals to participate and contribute to the economy, while also ensuring that everyone benefits from economic growth and prosperity.

This is a pretty inspiring definition and one where I don't have much disagreement. There are several key features of an inclusive economy:

- There is equal access to opportunity

- There is a level playing field

- There are shared benefits

The ChatGPT definition also highlights how these outcomes can be achieved, noting in particular fair taxation, equitable distribution of wealth, investment in infrastructure, and social programs. In other words, an inclusive economy requires the government to play its hand, along with other stakeholders.

Equal access to opportunity

Someone born in Manhattan in zip code 10007, which is Tribeca, is likely going to have very different life experiences than someone born to a family living in zip code 10456 in the Bronx (Mott Haven). What's the main difference between the two zip codes? Almost everything. These zip codes symbolize the extreme differences that exist in the same city: the richest zip code in the city compared to the poorest zip code in all five boroughs of New York City.

Starting with household incomes, the disparity is 10-fold between these two neighborhoods in New York City. Whereas median household income is just over $26K in Mott Haven, it is over $250K in Tribeca. There is a 10-year difference in life expectancy; a significant difference in education attainment; and a big difference in chronic disease. While of course, this data is not about causation, we can assume all sick people don't self-select and move to Mott Haven. It's more likely that the hardships that they experience in their life, including access to preventative healthcare, insurance, the resources to eat well and take care of themselves, are not as readily available to families earning $26K as compared to those earning ten times that amount.

Table 1: Key Indicators in different zip codes in New York

	Tribeca (zip code 10007)	Mott Haven (zip code 10456)
Mean household income	$512,350	$26,150
Median household income	$250,001+	$26,150
Life expectancy	85–86 years	76.7 years
Demographic	Predominantly white, some Asian; low poverty and unemployment rates.	Predominantly Hispanic and African American populations; high poverty and unemployment rates.
Education levels	A significant proportion of residents hold bachelor's degrees or higher.	Fewer residents with bachelor's degrees
Chronic disease	Low	High
Source:	*Forbes, NYU School of Global Public Health*	*NYU Furman Center, City Limits*

And what determines who lives in Tribeca and who lives in Mott Haven? Is it something intrinsic about these groups of people? In the 17th Century, many Europeans justified their colonial conquests of other countries by claiming that indeed, there were biological differences between whites and indigenous peoples of Africa, Asia, and Latin America. This justified their conquests as they were seen as bringing civilization to the uncivilized regions of the world. While this type of racism has been largely discredited by modern science, it is not completely gone from modern life. There are many remnants of colonialist thinking and race-based discrimination alive and well today.

In our scenario in New York, what distinguishes who lives in which neighborhood is primarily where they were born and who their parents were. Children born into wealthy households are more likely to live in places like Tribeca. Whereas children born in poor households are more likely to live in places like Mott Haven. These disparities stem not only from economic conditions but also from systemic inequalities that perpetuate cycles of poverty. Policies and historical practices such as redlining and discriminatory lending have long influenced which populations can afford to live in affluent neighborhoods and which are relegated to areas with fewer resources. Even today, gentrification continues to reshape urban landscapes, often displacing low-income families and further reinforcing segregation along socio-economic lines.

One's zip code can determine many things about them, including:

Health and Life Expectancy. Studies show that zip codes can have a strong correlation with health outcomes and life expectancy. Factors like access to quality healthcare, nutritious food, and safe environments can vary greatly between zip codes, leading to disparities in health. There are fewer hospitals in low-income neighborhoods.[98] There are often food deserts or not enough grocery stores that carry fresh fruits and vegetables.

---

[98] National Community Reinvestment Coalition (NCRC), *Your Zip Code Is More Important than Your Genetic Code* (NCRC, June 2021).

Without nutritious food, these communities are more likely to rely on poor quality food and experience obesity and other diet-related illness.[99]

Education and Opportunities. Zip codes often determine school districts, which can significantly impact educational opportunities and resources available to students. This can influence future career paths, earning potential, and overall social mobility.[100]

Safety. Living in a low-income neighborhood also entails a greater likelihood of crime and violence and increased police brutality.[101] Research by Johns Hopkins for the Center for Gun Violence Solutions at the School of Public Health shows that your zip code could increase your likelihood of getting shot by policy by 27 times. The study finds that in "2022 alone, an estimated 1,096 people were fatally shot by police in the U.S., and those individuals were disproportionately Black and Hispanic, male, or living in areas with high rates of unemployment and social vulnerability."[102]

Needless to say, if we want to create a society where everyone has equal access to opportunity, we must address the systems at play that keep people locked into the zip code in which they were born and that continues to influence every step of their life, including their life expectancy. This book will take us through what addressing this might mean for any society, not just the U.S.

Level playing field

Imagine your name is Shakir Rodriguez, and you were born in Mott Haven in the Bronx. Despite all of the odds, you graduate from college, the first to do so in your family.

---

[99] Ver Ploeg, Michele et al. *Mapping Food Deserts in the U.S.* (USDA Amber Waves, December 2011).
[100] Walker, Aswad, *Zip Codes: A Huge Determinant of Student Access to Educational Resources (*Defender Network, February 2022).
[101] School of Public Health, *New Research Shows Your ZIP Code Could Make You 27 times More Likely to be Fatally Shot by Police* (Johns Hopkins, October 2024).
[102] ibid

You start to apply for jobs, and what do you think will happen? Will your name trigger curiosity and interest, and will you be among the top candidates, or will your name trigger rejection?

A study in the U.S. by Bertrand and Mullainathan involved sending out identical resumes but with different names. White sounding names like Emily or Greg and African American sounding names like Lakisha and Jamal. Not surprisingly, White-sounding names received 50 percent more callbacks than those with African American-sounding names.[103]

These biases extend globally. In Sweden, a study by Erlandsson found that both male and female recruiters were more likely to contact applicants with Swedish-sounding names over those with foreign-sounding names. Notably, male applicants with foreign-sounding names faced greater discrimination than their female counterparts.[104] In India, a study by the LedBy Foundation found that identical qualifications but different names: one Hindu-sounding ("Priyanka Sharma") and one Muslim-sounding ("Habiba Ali"), revealed that Hindu-named individuals received nearly double the positive responses. The net discrimination rate was 47.1 percent, with higher bias observed in South and West India.[105] Creating a level playing field doesn't mean that everyone needs to name their children Emily and Greg to avoid this kind of discrimination. It requires that an anti-discrimination policy is in place and monitored to ensure that companies, government, and civil society all abide by the principles of fair access to employment.

Later in this book we'll cover the kind of policies that are essential for creating a level playing field.

[103] Paradis, Tim, *Emily or Lakisha*: Guess which one hiring managers chose? (Business Insider, April 2024).
[104] Erlandsson, Anni, *Gendered ethnic discrimination and the role of recruiter gender. A field experiment,* (Sage Journals, Volume 67, Issue 2, September 2023).
[105] Shadab, R., Sharan, V., & Lahiri, D., *Hiring Bias: Employment for Muslim Women at Entry-Level Roles.* (LedBy Foundation, 2022).

Shared benefits

> "Shared benefits refer to the fair and mutual gains derived from collaborative efforts, such as joint investments, policy agreements, or the management of shared resources."
>
> — *UNESCAP (2015), Framework for Regional Cooperation on Shared Natural Resources*

The concept of shared benefits is important because it says that equal access is insufficient for different individuals to benefit from an intervention, policy, or opportunity. Society should not stop at access but also needs to ensure that outcomes are achievable by different segments in society.

For physical barriers, this is perhaps easier to see. If access to a park requires climbing 100 stairs, then many segments of society may not be able to benefit from the park. Individuals in wheelchairs, someone with a physical injury, or an elderly person may not be able to benefit from the public goods that are available and paid for by public resources, such as the park in question. In this scenario, shared benefits mean that the public goods need to consider the barriers that certain segments may encounter and address these barriers in the design of the park. This could include a passage with a gradual incline for wheelchairs, building an escalator, or an elevator.

For barriers that are not visible, but which may still present insurmountable hurdles for some segments, this requires more work to uncover what these potential barriers might be and design solutions that take those into account. Imagine an adult who has never learned to use a smartphone or a computer. They are very comfortable using feature phones to make calls and even write texts. But they never made the transition to a smartphone nor tablets or computers. Now imagine this person goes to register for social security benefits and they must fill out a form online before they can speak to a person. Or imagine they are in a grocery store and there are only self-checkouts. To this person, the modern world appears inhospitable and insurmountable.

Increasingly, as our world is digitalizing, some segments are left behind. We need to ensure this transition benefits everyone, not just the privileged or those who are tech native.

Who is responsible? How does an inclusive economy come about?

There are many stakeholders who have a role to play in creating a world where everyone has the opportunity to participate and to benefit. It's impossible to imagine this world without the government playing an important role. Governments are service providers – whether we're talking about social security, healthcare, driver's licenses, passports, payroll for government workers, or the many ways in which governments offer direct-to-consumer or business services.

Governments are also essential in putting in place the rules by which the private sector operates. So, governments create an enabling environment for inclusive economies in the types of policies and regulations they enact, the agencies that oversee the work of the private sector, and the actions they take when actors are not abiding by the rules. Most importantly, governments play an essential role in setting guidelines for education, taxation, and labor standards. These form the critical environment that determines how equal a society is and whether benefits are distributed. The tools available to governments will be further explored in Chapter 8 and 9.

Working closely with the government in many developing countries are the development donors, like bilateral and multilateral agencies and philanthropic foundations. These actors can bring global knowledge, technical assistance, catalytic capital, and other support to governments as they embark on the path toward an inclusive digital economy. We touch on the role of development cooperation in Chapter 10.

The private sector, whether formal or informal, is the main employer in most economies, and thus it also plays a critical role in ensuring the services it offers are not inadvertently excluding certain groups.

As employers, the private sector must also ensure that their own internal practices and policies do not discriminate or unintentionally harm certain groups in society. Increasingly, businesses need to show their commitment to social good in order to compete for and retain their workforce. In Chapter 6, we'll discuss how inclusion is actually good for the business bottom line.

Many other players, like civil society organizations, community-based organizations, research organizations, non-profits, and others, also play a role as advocates, knowledge centers, watchdogs, and partners with both the public and private sectors in testing and scaling inclusive solutions (See chapter 11).

Chapter 5

Countering Entitlement & Backlash

In one of my previous jobs, there was a white woman from an aristocratic family in Europe. Let's call her Jane. Jane often received special treatment compared to other employees who came from a minority or non-European lineage. Jane's entitled attitude was noticeable compared to that of other employees. She consistently assumed her needs would be met by those around her. Decades before the pandemic, she received special permission to work from home. She was also the only person in the organization who had been allowed to work part-time - something considered a special privilege as part-time positions counted as full-time positions against tight headcount limitations.

At one stage, a young woman of non-European lineage, let's call her Mona, asked to get the same option to work part-time after having a baby. Because of the headcount limitations they asked both employees to submit their formal requests for part-time accommodation in writing. Managers reviewed the requests and authorized Mona to work part-time, given that Jane had already received that privilege for five consecutive years. Jane's anger at not getting what she wanted was noteworthy. She went on a rampage, denouncing the managers, denouncing the process, making accusations of discrimination, and claims of unfairness.

This, despite being a woman who had experienced nothing but privilege up to this point. She could only see her own needs and had never put herself in anyone else's shoes.

As an outsider, it was easy to see how privilege was playing out. Jane saw her rights being taken away. She was completely unaware of the privilege she experienced in the first place. It had become 'her right.'

This anecdote is just one example of how privilege and entitlement play out. Every day, as minority groups gain rights and spaces that they had previously been denied, the majority, or those who were accustomed to privilege, see their 'rights' being infringed upon. While I begin this chapter with an example about a woman's experience with privilege relating to race, the dominant privilege that transcends every country today is the privilege men enjoy relating to their gender.

What is privilege?

Privilege is the suite of benefits that people who are in the dominant group receive, not because of their own initiative, but simply because they are part of the dominant group. It is often invisible to the majority group. Privilege manifests in simple and complex ways.[106] It could be that when you enter a room, people don't stare at you. Or when you walk down the street, people don't cross to the other side. At work, it could be the holidays that you celebrate are the ones that are officially recognized. It could be that what you like to do socially – say play golf or drink beer – are the activities that are most supported during work retreats or happy hours with your colleagues.

In any society, there are dominant groups that maintain privilege and other groups that are perceived as less than. In India, religion is the main differentiator between groups, with Hindus representing the dominant group and other religions falling into the 'other' or 'less than' groups.

---

[106] Schwiter, Karen, *Male privilege revisited: How men in female-dominated occupations notice and actively reframe privilege* (Wiley, July 2021).

In France, white Catholics are the dominant group, and North African Muslims are the 'others'. In the U.S., whites are in the majority, and minority groups like Blacks, Latinx, Asians, Arabs, and many others, are in the minority. The dominant group can be a religious group, an ethnic group, a racial group, or some intersectional combination.

Who has privilege?

Privilege is often invisible to those who have it. They have never been 'the other' and thus the first time they don't benefit from what they are accustomed to feels like discrimination. In dominant culture, privilege is seeing your likeness represented on TV, in movies, in advertisements, and in positions of power and leadership. When someone who is different from you enters these spaces, the dominant culture feels threatened. The feeling that 'others' are 'trying to replace us' takes hold. This is what is termed The Great Replacement Theory, the belief among the extreme right in the U.S. that there is a plot to reduce the role of whites in the United States.[107]

A white woman I know who was interviewing for the role of CEO in a corporate foundation was not selected, and a woman of color was chosen as the president of the foundation. How did the white woman see this selection? Her first reaction was that the person selected only got the role because of her color. She felt she had experienced 'reverse racism.' To her, no other factors were ever considered for this selection. She was incapable of reflecting on her poor relationships inside the organization, her negative attitude toward leadership, her vision for the role, which did not align with the priorities of the corporation or her own skill set. She immediately explained the selection as color based.

In the U.S., white society is the dominant culture and thus the most prevalent noticeable privilege is that experienced by white people.

---

[107] Bauder, David, *What is the great replacement theory and how does it fuel racist violence* (PBS News, May 2022).

The examples of privilege are so pervasive, it's impossible to cover them all. A few notable examples include:

- White school districts received $23 billion more funding compared to non-white school districts, even while serving the same number of students.[108]

- When looking to buy property in the U.S., white people are consistently shown more home options than people of color, even if they have the same financial profiles.

- White sounding names are more likely to get selected for an interview than non-white sounding names. According to a study by Marianne Bertrand and Sendhil Mullainathan, people with white sounding names needed to send out 10 resumes to get a response, whereas those with traditionally black sounding names had to send out 15 resumes. This is a 50 percent gap in callback rates for black people for the same jobs, with equal qualifications.[109]

In much of the world, the dominant group is based on gender. Men are more likely to experience privilege than women or any other gender.

Brian Lowery, a professor at Stanford University, discusses a system of privilege that is maintained by a process of identity management called the three D's: Deny, Distance, Dismantle.[110]

---

[108] https://edbuild.org/content/23-billion
[109] National Bureau of Economic Research, *Employers' Replies to Racial Names* (NBER The Digest, September 2023).
[110] Knowles ED, Lowery BS, Chow RM, Unzueta MM. *Deny, Distance, or Dismantle? How White Americans Manage a Privileged Identity* (Perspect Psychol Sci., November 2014).

The psychology behind the three D's is that they help make the person feel like a moral person and help to explain their gains in life through meritocracy, not through unseen privilege. It is uncomfortable to explain personal gains due to anything other than meritocracy. Often, dominant groups use the psychological tactic of denying privilege in the first place. Denying privilege often comes by highlighting the hardships that an individual faces.

The second tactic often used is distancing oneself from the privilege. For example, segregation between races or groups creates 'herd invisibility.' If enough people are experiencing the same thing, then one's own privilege does not exist. Your experience becomes the norm.

Research by Karin Schwiter, Julia Nentwich, and Marisol Keller explores how men who work in female-dominated fields justify the privileges they experience. Their research reveals that men in female-dominated occupations notice their privilege and acknowledge receiving preferential treatment. However, rather than contesting this privilege, they employ discursive strategies to justify and silence it. They use one of two ways to address their privilege: the first involves emphasizing the features of the male body as an asset, while the second involves highlighting individual performance and competencies to justify preferential treatment. These strategies allow men to reframe privilege as a legitimate achievement and silence the "patriarchal dividend."[111]

In May 2023, the world surpassed an important milestone. There were more women S&P 500 CEOs than CEOs named John.[112] There are 41 female CEOs leading S&P 500 companies; only 23 CEOs named John are in this S&P 500 CEO cohort. As women finally advance in leadership roles, however, men are experiencing a sense of loss.

---

[111] Schwiter, Karen et al. *Male privilege revisited: How men in female-dominated occupations notice and actively reframe privilege* (Wiley, 2021).
[112] Terrell, Cynthia Richie, *Women CEOs Finally Outnumber CEOs Named John; Washington State Could Get a Woman Governor* (Ms. Magazine, May 2023).

Recently, a Swiss Nobel Laureate by the name of Kurt Wüthrich claimed that he experienced 'male discrimination' during the 72nd Lindau Nobel Laureate meeting.[113] His evidence to support this included the request by the photographer that women stand in front and men stand in the back while taking the meeting photo.[114]

The actual data, that men account for 89 Nobel prizes as compared to only 60 women evaded his logic.

Inevitable backlash

There is abundant evidence of a backlash against women for the real or perceived gains that they have had over the past decades. This backlash is central to the 'exchange of power' from those who were born with it to those who may be newly acquiring it. Eventually, backlash happens to all groups that are gaining power from those who perceive themselves as ceding power.[115]

Research by Cecilia Hyunjung Mo at Berkeley finds evidence throughout history that when groups experience a sense of being left behind, they can create destabilizing tendencies in society. She points out that "If you've been accustomed to being at the top — if that's what you've known, how you've been socialized, and what history has taught you — then it is not unreasonable for you to start assuming that, "We're supposed to be at the top." As a consequence, if you start believing that there are other groups surpassing you, doing better than you think your group is doing, then it makes sense that you start feeling discontent."[116]

[113] Robinson, Julia, *Nobel laureate speaks of experiencing 'male discrimination' at annual Lindau meeting* (Chemistry World, June 2023).
[114] Bilal, Mushtaq (X Post, July 2, 2023).
https://twitter.com/MushtaqBilalPhD/status/1675419994195148807?lang=en
[115] Townsend-Bell, Erica. *Backlash as the Moment of Revelation* (Signs, Winter 2020).
[116] Lempinen, Edward, *Cecilia Hyunjung Mo: The male backlash against democracy is no surprise* (UC Berkely News, November 18, 2022).

The sense of loss also emanates from high expectations that are not being met. If you are accustomed to being on top and being listened to, then when a situation arises and you are not on top, but just one of many voices, there is growing discomfort with the status quo. The idea that all voices are equal and that you must defer to the views of others may not align with the role you expected of yourself. It can be particularly egregious if you are now having to report to someone of color in the workplace or merely have to listen to someone who does not look like you.

Typically, the backlash comes as a result of norms around acceptable behaviors for different segments of society. The gender backlash is typically associated with women behaving in a way that is not feminine enough.[117] For example, in my own life, I've been questioned by a previous boss about my confidence and why I am not more deferential. By behaving differently than the normative expectations of your gender, class, race, religion, or other characteristics, you often experience economic and social penalties or what is often discussed as sanctions against this behavior. These sanctions may manifest in gossip about your behavior, judgment about your personality, limitations to your 'potential' as an employee if you do not fit a specific character mold, and so on.

The backlash can also come in more subtle ways by consistently shifting the goalpost when it comes to women. I distinctly remember a conversation at a leadership team meeting where a young Asian woman's promotion was being discussed, and several men among the senior leadership noted her 'lack of gravitas.' To avoid giving her a promotion, a new set of behavioral and work achievements were set which were more onerous than what was required for male colleagues.

Different racial groups are dealing with different stereotypes and cultural expectations, which result in different experiences linked to gender backlash.

---

[117] Xiao, Vivian. *Gender Backlash and the Paradox of Race* (SPSS blog, July 17, 2023).

Research has shown that the race of the target woman and the race of the evaluator plays a role. And counter to expectations, judgement of 'in-group' may be more severe than that of the 'out-group.' In other words, black women may judge other black women more harshly than a white woman if her behavior doesn't align with expectations around black women. As expectations of white women may be different, there may be less backlash against white women for any perceived misbehavior.[118]

Moving toward equity and inclusion

The process to move toward greater equity for all people is to recognize privilege where it lies. This means real work for those who have never experienced anything other than privilege. To a certain extent, everyone has experienced some form of privilege based on their sex, size, religion, or some other factor. Starting with recognizing where you may have experienced privilege is helpful, but this is difficult work for most people to do on their own.

One way to approach the concept of privilege without triggering a rejection of the idea or defensiveness is to use an indirect channel to try to elicit privileged experiences from those who have no awareness of it. For example, rather than asking someone directly how they experience privilege as a white man or as a white woman, the question can be approached indirectly by asking, "Was your success down to luck or your skills?"[119] Bringing in 'luck' into the equation opens up the opportunity for discussions around the 'luck' you may have had being born into a middle class or wealthy family, or the 'luck' of being born in the U.S. or Europe rather than in a conflict-affected country, or that you lived in a community where public schools provided a reasonably good education, or a myriad of other 'lucky' factors that have given you an advantage over others. This kind of discussion doesn't begin with the issues of race, religion, or gender, but can eventually lead to a discussion of how your situation may have influenced your ability to access the opportunities you

---

[118] Townsend-Bell, Erica. *Backlash as the Moment of Revelation* (Signs, Winter 2020).
[119] See work by Cassi Mecchi

accessed. This then opens up the door to raising awareness of privilege. When people begin to acknowledge that privilege exists, they are more open to policy solutions that aim to level the playing field. When people feel better about themselves, they are also more likely to affirm the experience of others.

Engagement with dominant groups

Moving toward greater equity cannot be achieved without engagement with the groups that have historically benefited from privilege. This inevitably means a need to focus on men and boys. There is a long history of understanding this for those working on feminist activism. In certain fields, like global health, working with men and boys is also fundamental to addressing persistent gender-based health injustices such as gender-based violence, female genital mutilation, or child marriage.

In fact, gender equality can only truly happen when men's attitudes and behaviors change radically. "Engaging men in advancing gender equality is often positioned as a 'win-win'. While men have an ethical responsibility to change the systems that grant them power and privilege, they will also gain from doing so, in terms of their well-being, their relational interests, and the benefits to the communities in which they live. Gender equality can be transformational for men through their greater participation in care, more holistic experiences of fatherhood, more equal and fulfilling intimate partner relations, and closer relationships to dependents."[120]

'Engagement' refers to the practice of involving or addressing men, while accountability refers to how it must be done. At its most basic level, accountability to women means that women's and girls' human rights should be at the center of the work with men, and deep collaboration, engagement, and dialogue with women's organizations is essential. This means accountability to eliminate discrimination against women and girls by actively contributing to changes in attitudes, norms, systems, and

---

[120] OHCHR. *Men's Accountability for Gender Equality* (UN Human Rights Special Procedures OHCHR, December 2022).

structures and gender roles across all spheres. While the principle of accountability is widely endorsed among actors working with men and boys to advance gender equality, particularly in men's anti-violence work, its practice is more uneven.

Dismantling concepts of toxic masculinity

Engaging men often means also tackling concepts around toxic masculinity that are harmful for men as well as society at large. Toxic masculinity is the set of ideas around how men should behave: stoical, unemotional, macho, and strong. Men who do not conform are often mistreated by both men and women. By learning as boys to hide or bury their emotions, boys can grow up without ever fully experiencing important feelings that are part of the human experience. Boys are shaped to fit into a tight box of what it means to be a man. Without the full gamut of feelings, boys can quickly turn to violence as they may lack the emotional skills to process feelings or resolve conflicts.

In her book, Feminist Theory: From Margin to Center, feminist theorist and author, Bell Hooks, wrote, "The first act of violence that patriarchy demands of males is not violence toward women. Instead, patriarchy demands of all males that they engage in acts of psychic self-mutilation, that they kill off the emotional parts of themselves. If an individual is not successful in emotionally crippling himself, he can count on patriarchal men to enact rituals of power that will assault his self-esteem."[121]

Resetting the concept of masculinity is best achieved through a fundamental shift in how boys are raised and the role of fathers in the household.[122] There is a great deal of emerging research that discusses the need for young boys to acknowledge and express their feelings, and that traditional parenting, which engages the feelings of girls but asks boys not to exhibit their feelings, is the root cause of men who are not emotionally evolved.

---

[121] Kindman and Company, *On toxic masculinity* (Kindman & Co Blog, April 2011).
[122] Marschall, Garin, *As Fathers, We Must Commit to Dismantling the Patriarchy* (Yes Magazine, July 4, 2019).

An article in the Atlantic notes, "sons need the same nurturing that many parents so naturally bestow on daughters: time, conversation, patience, and affection. In fact, they might need it more... boys get less tender nurturing than girls do, or the care that they receive tends to emphasize physical activity over more intimate emotional interactions."[123]

Creating allyships

Who can do this work? I have found that in my own life experience as a brown woman, my voice is not accepted in the same way as that of a white man's. While it is enormously frustrating that I must work through others to be heard, I have found that sometimes it is the only way to communicate with the dominant culture. Otherwise, the backlash is very much the only thing you will experience. This means that people from the dominant culture are needed to speak to others in the dominant culture.

Allyship means using "an active and consistent effort to use your privilege and power to support and advocate for people with less privilege."[124] To be an ally, one must first recognize the inequities that are prevalent, whether in the workplace or at the grocery store. This involves taking action when inequities are visible in daily interactions.

One example of this happening in real time involved an attack on the metro in London on a young girl who happened to be veiled. A man in his 30's started to attack her and called her a terrorist. Another young man instantaneously stepped in between them and then sat next to the girl to distract her and protect her.[125] While this may seem so insignificant, it is surprisingly uncommon.

---

[123] Coleman, Joshua, *What Parents of Boys Should Know* (The Atlantic, April 30, 2025).
[124] Lean In, *Allyship at Work* (Accessed July 2025).
[125] Al-Othman, Hannah, *Man intervenes to stop racist attack on woman on Tube 'provoked by Paris attacks'* (The Standard, November 17, 2015).

Harassment, on the other hand, is quite common: it's estimated that 71 percent of women have experienced harassment in public spaces.[126]

We have a long way to go to help people learn to step in when harassment is in action.

Support policies to redistribute resources

While individuals have a role to play, reflecting on themselves and serving as allies, the work must go further than this. To address the systemic injustices that perpetuate privileges for some and inequality for others, ultimately, government and other institutions need to step in with policies that address the fundamental inequalities and put in place sanctions for those who perpetrate injustices.

The picture below has been modified and shared across social media for a long time now. It's brilliance is how easily it explains the concepts of privilege (the reality scenario), the concept of equality (which gives everyone the same set of tools, but doesn't account for their starting endowments), and the concept of equity which aims to address these underlying endowments to enable everyone to participate fully in society and the economy.

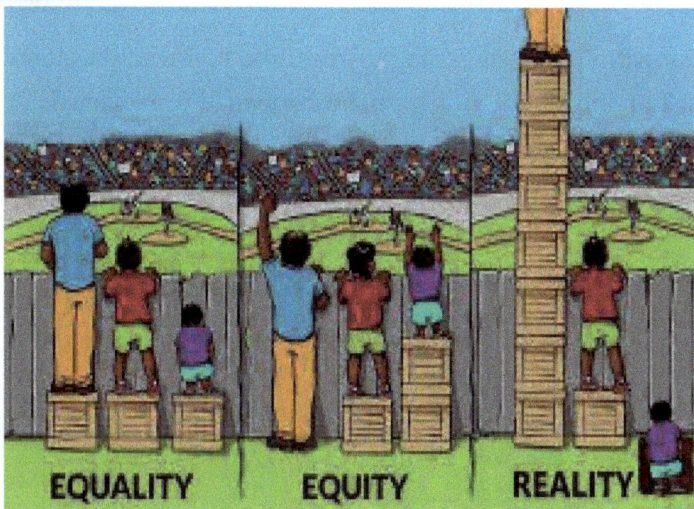

---

[126] Avon and Somerset Police, *If not you, then who? How to be an active bystander when someone is being harassed* (Avon and Somerset Police, December 2023).

In the workplace, it's easy to see how creating equity can be achieved by ensuring that those who may have specific disabilities are accommodated or by ensuring that caregivers are provided the protections they need to manage their care responsibilities alongside their work.

Similar accommodation can be made for access to health care, education, or work.

Policies that are about discrimination are important, but not enough. Discrimination gets us to equality but doesn't get us to equity. Examples of policies that address systemic inequality include the UK's Disability Discrimination Act.[127] The Act requires that barriers that prevent people with disabilities from accessing services or participating in the workforce be removed. The Act covers employment (working conditions, training, hiring, etc.); access to services like shops, banks, and public transport; education; and renting or buying property. To enforce the Act, the Disability Rights Commission (DRC) was created and has since been integrated into the broader Equality and Human Rights Commission (EHRC).[128]

What does this all mean for the digital economy?

Many of the barriers we've discussed in earlier chapters, whether that is what women experience with a lack of access to mobile phones or internet, or the added harassment or abuse they experience when engaging with the digital financial sector, are part of this broader story of privilege and backlash. When thinking about solutions for addressing these barriers, we can't simply put a band-aid on such gaping wounds.

Handing out a phone to a poor, urban woman is not going to solve her access to the digital economy. It will trigger backlash against what may be perceived as her gained power and independence.

---

[127] UK Government, Disability Discrimination Act 1995
[128] https://www.equalityhumanrights.com

Giving a rural farmer internet will not mean that she will be able to translate that into reshaping her role in the rural economy. What will the local merchants do? What will her husband do? How can we ensure that the little power she gets from connectivity is not used against her?

If we are in the business of supporting a digital economy, we cannot escape the responsibility to address the reaction that comes with every action. We must look at barriers and solutions comprehensively as we seek to address equity and inclusion in the digital economy. In the next chapters, we will shift the discussion to how this can be done at a systems level, and not just one person at a time.

Chapter 6

Inclusion is Good for Business

Lack of inclusion can hurt the bottom line

In 2019, the online home furniture giant, Wayfair, saw its employees walk out in protest over the sale of furniture to an immigrant detention center near the U.S.-Mexico border. The letter, signed by employees, stated that the U.S. government's actions and its contractors did not align with their values, nor did this engagement represent an ethical business partnership for Wayfair. The company acknowledged the letter and the sentiment but proceeded to fulfill its contractual obligations to the U.S. Government.

In the same year, over 4,000 employees at Amazon signed a letter demanding that the company take more action to combat climate change. Employees demanded firm commitment from the company to reduce its emissions in its distribution network. While the company has taken measures to address the emissions from within its distribution network, management has fought efforts at the board level to increase its reporting and accountability on efforts to combat climate change.

The U.S.'s largest employer, Walmart, faced similar employee actions. Around 50,000 employees signed a petition objecting to the sale of firearms and ammunition in Walmart stores. The petition demanded that the company not only stop the sale of arms, but also ban open carry-on properties, and stop donations to the NRA.

The company did take measures to address employee concerns by discontinuing the sale of handguns and some rifles. However, it continues to sell arms and ammunition for hunting.[129]

Beyond employee activism, research shows that actions taken by CEOs can result in consumers changing their purchasing decisions. In 2018, a survey by the Rock Center for Corporate Governance found that if a customer disagrees with a decision made by a CEO on social or political issues, they are more likely to switch products to companies where they agree with the stance of the CEO.[130]

But how does a company avoid this conundrum? Needless to say, it is impossible to please everyone, but clearly companies must do more to align their values with their employees and customers. And this starts with leadership resembling the people they serve.

Diversity is still a challenge for many companies

It is troubling, then, that the data on corporate leadership shows that very little progress has been achieved in recent years, despite efforts to reshape leadership to be more representative. The starkest example of this lack of representation is in the absurd fact that until recently, there were more men named John in CEO positions than the entire category of female leaders.[131] In 2018, there were only 23 women in CEO positions in the U.S., and 25 men named John, according to research by the *New York Times*.

---

[129] Larcker, David F. et al., *Protests from Within: Engaging with Employee Activists* (Harvard Law School Forum on Corporate Governance, March 24, 2021).
[130] Rock Center for Corporate Governance at Stanford University, *2018 CEO Activism Survey* (Stanford University, 2018).
[131] Bonazzo, John, *Men Named John Outnumber All Women in Most American Industries* (Observer, April 2018).

BCG's research shows many other troubling signs of highly concentrated leadership and ineffective efforts to achieve progress with diversity, equity and inclusion (DEI) initiatives. Their data shows that:

- White, straight men dominate. A whopping 90 percent of the CEOs of Fortune 500 companies are white, straight men.

- 75 percent of employees are not experiencing the benefits of DEI initiatives.

- And, a very high number of employees, 55 percent, are still experiencing some form of discrimination in the workplace. [132]

McKinsey has been monitoring performance of top companies with regard to gender and ethnic diversity in leadership teams since 2015. Its most recent report, published in 2020, finds that diversity matters more than ever, and COVID has had a further impact on this overall trend. Diverse companies outperform their industry peers with regard to profitability. And yet, research shows that progress is not linear. Only 33 percent of the firms that McKinsey tracked continue to progress with increasing diversity and inclusion, with the remaining stalling or even slipping further behind. With recent anti-DEI backlash, this is likely to worsen in the coming years.

In its research covering 15 countries and more than 1,000 companies, McKinsey finds that more diverse companies outperform those with non-diverse leadership.[133] Performance is highest with companies that have greater ethnic diversity in leadership, followed by gender diversity. Companies with greater ethnic diversity in leadership outperform peers by 36 percent. Their research also shows that board diversity has an impact. Companies with more diverse boards are 28 percent more likely to outperform peer companies.

---

[132] BCG, *It's Time to Reimagine Diversity, Equity and Inclusion* (Boston Consulting Group, May 2021).
[133] McKinsey, *Diversity Wins: How Inclusion Matters* (McKinsey, May 2020).

Beyond the bottom line, diverse companies are more innovative

In addition to producing financial results for companies, diversity and inclusion have many other benefits. They have longer-term effects that can influence a company's competitiveness and growth. One of the areas that perhaps has the most strategic significance is helping companies keep up with innovation by staying more attuned to opportunities and risks as they emerge. Diversity achieves this as it helps to flag how different segments of society may react to or perceive new products, brands, advertisements, and other essential corporate identifiers.

In 2023, during a war between Israel and Hamas, with daily images of enormous physical and human losses, Zara launched a campaign that appeared to depict destruction (see image below). The model is carrying a mannequin wrapped in white plastic, mirroring the many images coming out of Gaza with families carrying their murdered children wrapped in white sheets. Zara received so much backlash on the campaign that it had to pull it and then apologize for the gaffe.[134] Stories like this raise the question as to who was at the decision-making table when this campaign was launched. Had there been a more diverse set of leaders, perhaps such a gaffe would not have been so inevitable.

---

[134] See https://www.theguardian.com/fashion/2023/dec/12/zara-pulls-uk-ad-campaign-images-gaza and
https://www.washingtonpost.com/business/2023/12/12/zara-gaza-ad-campaign-boycott/

Fashion brand says it regrets 'misunderstanding' over photos taken before start of conflict

📷 Kristen McMenamy holds a mannequin wrapped in white plastic in the Zara ad campaign, which was photographed before the Israel-Gaza war. Photograph: Zara

Research by Boston Consulting Group finds that diverse management is more likely to see financial results from innovation. Diversity, along all ranks in the company and not just at the top, allows companies to address challenges, take more calculated risks, and take advantage of challenging situations and turn them into opportunities more creatively. BCG finds that in response to changing consumer preferences, diverse companies can make more radical decisions by introducing more innovative responses. They are also able to better predict and respond to shifting consumer preferences, again more likely because they are more representative of the people to whom they are catering.

Figure 1: Companies with more diverse leadership teams report higher innovation revenue

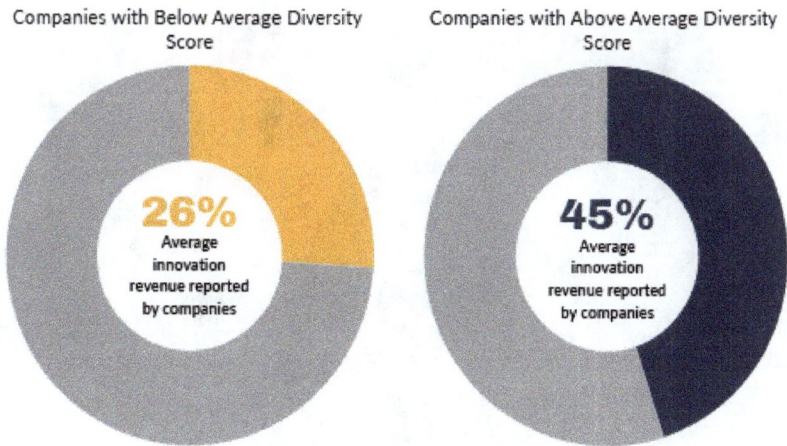

Companies with Below Average Diversity Score

26%
Average innovation revenue reported by companies

Companies with Above Average Diversity Score

45%
Average innovation revenue reported by companies

Source: BCG

People who all look alike and have a shared lived experience are more likely to agree and see things from the same angle. It is no surprise that boards or managers who are predominantly white are more at risk of what's often called 'groupthink.' Homogeneity, especially at the top, can lead to complete blindness to the experience of people not from the dominant group.[135]

Diversity is not just about gender and race; it can also encompass work experience, age, educational background, cognitive abilities, place of origin, and maybe even management style. While many managers hire people who look like and think like them, this can lead to worse outcomes.

I recently witnessed the harmful effects that cognitive similarity and 'groupthink' can have even within what appears to be a shared demographic group.

---

[135] Tsusaka, Miki et al., *Winning the '20s: Business imperative of diversity* (BCG Hendersen Institute, June 2019).

A group of women who had been used to a specific style of leadership that rewarded loyalty and harmony struggled to adapt to a new leader who had a different style of leadership, which was more direct and focused on accountability toward results. The group bonded against the new leader, claiming they felt unsafe in this new environment. They felt that the new leader's focus on accountability, raising questions about behaviors and actions that had previously been condoned, such as securing favors from the leader, even against company policy, was threatening and, in turn, felt unsafe. The fact that many of the underlying actions that these women were undertaking were themselves the problem, such as traveling without authorization, seeking privileges without formal approval, and making hiring decisions without discussion, was beyond their comprehension. They had always been able to get what they wanted through the former leader, and a change in this is what felt unsafe to them. Someone challenging their 'privilege' was considered unsafe.

Inclusive organizations are more likely to have engaged staff

In most organizations, the staff is the engine to achieve the targeted financial results. It's hard to imagine a successful company without staff who are satisfied or engaged in their job. Inclusive organizations are more likely to lead to engaged staff, according to a study by Deloitte. When companies make announcements about diversity and inclusion and do not follow through, or do so only performatively, then trust can erode between management and staff.

In a recent work experience, the leadership of the organization, which was made up of three white men from elite backgrounds, was often perplexed that staff did not believe the claims that they promoted diversity and inclusiveness. What staff witnessed was a dominant white culture that was set at the top. It was not surprising that people of color were consistently more unsatisfied with the organization, and despite efforts to fill the ranks with diverse staff, they were not likely to stay or be engaged.

Deloitte's research finds that when staff don't trust leadership, they are less engaged and less likely to perform at their best. Conversely, trust in leadership can result in up to 20 percent higher engagement, and departure or turnover can be reduced by 87 percent.[136]

Staff attitudes toward inclusion have only solidified since the pandemic and the ensuing 'Great Resignation.' Increasingly, employees are shifting their priorities and focusing more on living their values. When the values of their employers no longer align with their own, they are much more likely to leave and seek values alignment with other employers or go out on their own as independent workers.[137]

Company values can lead to customer (dis)loyalty

Increasingly, customers are voting with their proverbial pocketbooks, or perhaps more aptly with their Apple wallet. Surveys of consumer behaviors reveal that 55 percent of surveyed consumers were more likely to purchase items from companies where they felt alignment of values. Only 4 percent of consumers in the same survey felt that values did not affect their purchasing decisions. The areas consumers felt strongest about were pay equity and labor practices, where a whopping 73 percent of consumers listed it as very or extremely important. The environment came next with 71 percent of respondents noting it as very or extremely important, followed by racial equity at 68 percent.[138]

Increasingly, boycotts are a tool to force companies to change their support of unjust practices. Perhaps the most effective boycotts in our lifetime were those carried out against South Africa's apartheid. In the UK, one in four residents were boycotting South African products by the mid-1980's. South African artists were blocked from performing on the BBC as a result of pressure from the musician's union.

---

[136] Prabhakar, Kavitha et al, *Building trust in diversity, equity and inclusion commitments* (Deloitte Insights, 2022).
[137] ibid
[138] Carr, Pri, *Consumers Are Declaring Their Social Values Through Purchase Decisions—Are You Listening?* (AdWeek, Accessed July 2025).

In the U.S., the efforts focused primarily on divestment pressure at universities and churches; the pressure eventually forced the U.S. government to impose financial sanctions and divestment from South Africa.[139]

Most recently, companies that are perceived as supporting occupation or benefiting from human rights abuses in the West Bank and Gaza are seeing significant impacts and are forced to deal with consumer backlash.

The Palestinian movement goes under the banner of BDS, or Boycott, Divestment and Sanctions. It has affected McDonald's and Starbucks perhaps more than other companies. Israeli IDF soldiers were treated with free meals from the local franchisee of McDonald's, and this caused fury across the Middle East. Franchisee owners in other countries in the region, including Saudi Arabia, Oman, Kuwait, the UAE, Jordan, and Turkey, all responded by distancing themselves from the Israeli franchise. In some cases, the local franchisees have pledged aid to Gazan victims to compensate for the negative impact that the Israeli franchise has caused the brand.[140] Starbucks recently closed in Morocco due to low demand. Some say that this was a direct result of the boycott, while the company claims otherwise.[141]

Musicians and artists have refused to perform in Israel. There have even been cries for the Eurovision contest to exclude Israel due to its atrocities in Gaza.[142] While it is hard to measure the material effects of the BDS movement, one proxy is the social media prevalence and influence these campaigns have.

---

[139] McGreal, Chris, *Israel apartheid boycotts sanctions South Africa* (The Guardian, May 23, 2021).
[140] Magid, Pesha, *Free meals for Israeli soldiers divide McDonald's franchises* (Reuters, October 17, 2023).
[141] El Atti, Basma, *Starbucks and H&M close in Morocco over Gaza boycott, owners deny departure citing 'reorganization'* (The New Arab, December 1, 2023).
[142] Mouriquand, David, *Eurovision 2024: Nordic artists calling for Israel to be banned,* Euro News (January 16, 2024).

A hashtag on TikTok #boycottisrael achieved 340 million views two months after the war in Gaza. The hashtag #BDS has captured at least 3 billion views, also on TikTok.[143]

The viral effects of social media and the increasingly organized approaches that campaigns such as BDS are having are likely to continue; this is not a trend that companies can ignore. McKinsey notes that social decisions are now shaping consumer behaviors more than ever before. Companies need to align their values with their target markets if they intend to capture consumer loyalty and spending.[144] Research conducted by Harris Poll commissioned by Google Cloud finds that 82 percent of U.S. shoppers are demanding alignment of values with companies. Over 75 percent of shoppers reported that they changed brands as a result of conflicting values with a company.[145]

The value-driven purchasing trends are not limited to specific demographic groups and seem to cut across age, gender, and race. McKinsey researched what they term the 'inclusive consumer,' or the consumer who self-identifies as driven by social values and compared this to the 'normal' consumer in their demographic categories. They assessed their interest in supporting black-owned companies as one example of social motivation. Findings across age, gender, race, and region show that the 'inclusive consumer' and the 'normal' consumer are in much more alignment than would be expected. This demonstrates how viral or mainstream social attitudes have shifted, irrespective of one's awareness or self-identification.

---

[143] Vinal, Francis, *What's the BDS, the movement to boycott Israel with a new social media following* (The Washington Post, January 23, 2024).

[144] McKinsey and Company, *The rise of the inclusive consumer* (McKinsey and Company, February 8, 2022).

[145] Bounfantino, Giusy, *New Research Shows Consumers More Interested in Brands' Values than Ever* (Consumer Goods Technology, April 27, 2022).

Figure 2: Purchasing trends among consumers across demographics in the US

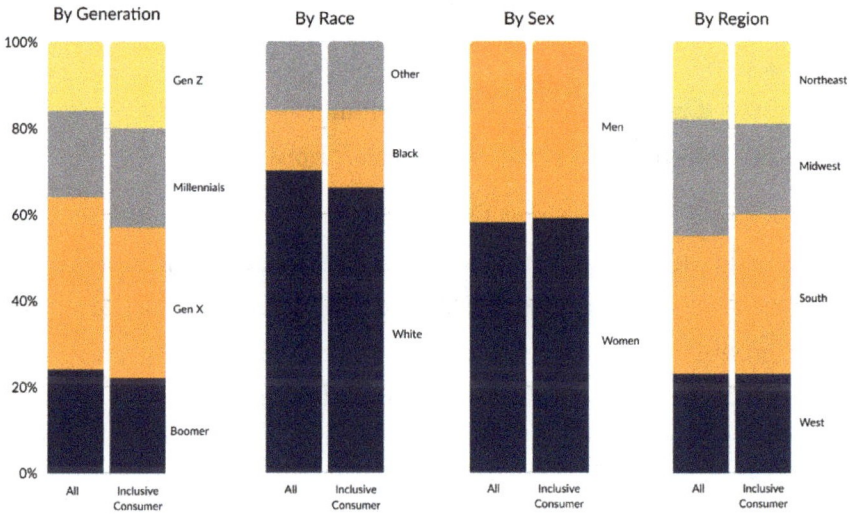

Source: McKinsey Inclusive Consumer Survey 2021

Add 'diversity and stir' is not enough

Hiring more diverse workers but not creating an environment where they can thrive means that companies are not benefitting from the full potential of diverse and inclusive cultures.[146] Bringing diverse voices to the table can initially lead to perceptions of conflicts, particularly if the dominant culture was more 'harmonious' in its decision-making processes. New people, who do not look like the majority, may be threatening to the dominant culture and may be targeted for 'not fitting in.'

While all the big firms have invested in diversity, equity, and inclusion initiatives, many of them have also experienced significant backlash from majority cultures.

---

[146] Tsusaka, Miki et al., *Winning the '20s: Business imperative of diversity* (BCG Hendersen Institute, June 2019).

87

Perhaps the most vocal and visible anti-DEI actor has been billionaire Bill Ackman, who led the attack against Harvard University President, Claudine Gay, which ultimately led to her resignation.

He has published a kind of manifesto on X which claims that DEI is "inherently a racist and illegal movement in its implementation even if it purports to work on behalf of the so-called oppressed."[147]

Research by BCG shows that DEI efforts are igniting backlash from the traditionally dominant, or majority groups. Figure 3 below shows that straight, cisgender men are more likely to feel that DEI is ineffective than other groups in both the UK and the U.S. These same groups also believe that these efforts are leading to greater inefficiency.

---

[147] Ackman, Bill (X Post, January 3, 2024).

Figure 3: By inadvertently excluding the majority DEI efforts can fuel divisiveness

Majority opinion of DEI initiatives if they feel excluded...

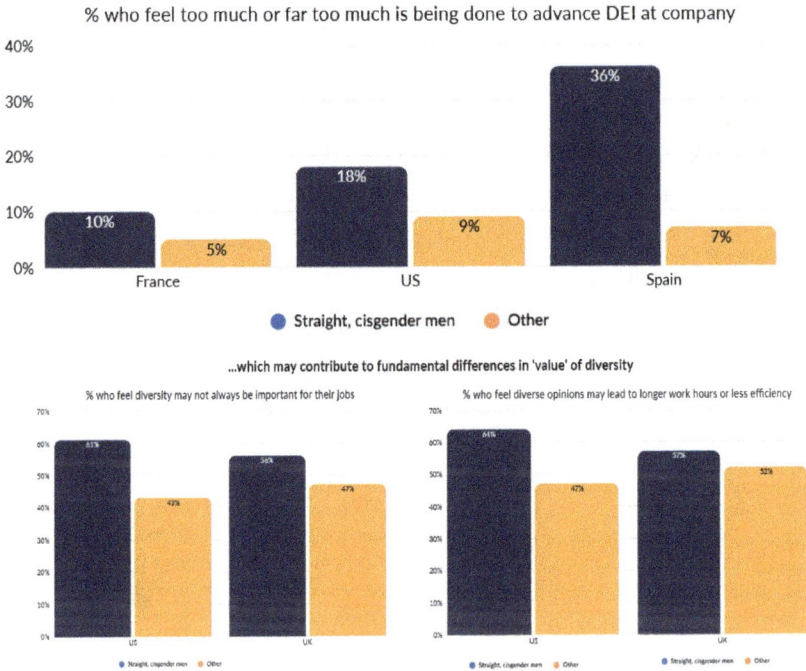

% who feel too much or far too much is being done to advance DEI at company

● Straight, cisgender men   ● Other

...which may contribute to fundamental differences in 'value' of diversity

Source: BGC. "It's time to reimagine diversity, equity and inclusion." May 2021

What does it take to create that environment, where everyone can thrive? Where both the historic majority as well as individuals who have systematically been excluded from the status quo can do well? There are no easy answers in today's polarized environment. Inevitably, it must start with leadership that is committed to the social changes that have begun but are far from over. Leaders at the governance and managerial levels must be open to hearing new voices, admitting their ignorance about the lived experiences of others, and allowing the sharing of power with those whom they previously dominated.

This will require leaders to look inward, get support, and acknowledge they can no longer rely on their instincts, which may be inherently built on privilege.

Beyond leadership, organizations will need policies and practices that allow divergent voices to emerge, and they must protect those who have unpopular voices, particularly if this aligns with differences such as race, religion, age, or place of origin. The old knee-jerk reaction to protect the comfort of the majority has no space in this time of historical reckoning.

A culture is not only made up of policies and procedures, but also of the line managers who often do not have the skills to manage the array of feelings, voices, and conflicts that will inevitably ensue. Organizations will need to provide support, not only to the leadership, but also to the line staff who are the frontline force that is responsible for creating a culture where everyone truly has a right to partake.

Chapter 7

Equal access to opportunity

The world is littered with development projects that had good intentions but somehow did not get traction. These 'solutions' were put in place to provide equal access to water, education, sanitation, or whichever development challenge was being addressed.

The Rural Agency for Sustainable Development in Gambia received computers and internet access to set up an internet café, but within just a few years, the café was non-operational, and computers went unused.[148]

The PlayPump, a playground merry-go-round that uses the energy from children playing to create energy and operate a water pump, was highly celebrated and endorsed by many celebrities, U.S. First Lady Laura Bush, and former U.S. President Bill Clinton. Yet, in the end, many were uninstalled.

In Rwanda, the government subsidized mobile phones hoping to increase uptake and adoption of mobile technology, particularly with women in rural areas. Research tracing usage leveraging transaction data from the phones found that the intended users, rural women, were not necessarily the ones who adopted the phones, as locations of the users

---

[148] https://en.wikipedia.org/wiki/Rural_Agency_for_Sustainable_Development

tended to migrate to urban centers, indicating either sale or gifting of the phones to other members of their households and networks.[149]

Where did these and thousands of similar initiatives go wrong?

Build it and they will come...not!

Most failed development efforts use the 'build it and they will come' mentality. They are so confident in the value of the solution that they never do their homework to understand the challenges that specific customer segments face. Nor do they think about what it takes to maintain the solution over time and what is needed from a financial or technical capacity perspective.

Many of these initiatives are potentially expensive to build and install, and in turn can be difficult to maintain without specific skills. Even more worrying, some may unintentionally create dependency on low-cost child labor, worsening conditions for the people who were meant to benefit. The 'build it and they will come' mentality rarely does the on-the-ground consultation necessary with the users and their communities to understand the society, gendered or physical barriers that may be real or perceived, which interfere with uptake and usage.

When it comes to the digital economy, as we've seen in Chapter 2, distributing mobile phones, even for free, won't necessarily mean that these phones will be valued, that the individuals receiving them will know how to use them or that the community will support girls or women to use phones or the internet on their own.

That mobile data is available doesn't mean that low-income people will use their meager earnings to get access to the internet, especially when they don't know how this will translate to meaningful change in their lives.

---

[149] Björkegren, Daniel and Ceyhun Karaca, Burak. *The Effect of Network Adoption Subsidies: Evidence from Digital Traces in Rwanda* (Cornell University, February 2020).

We have come to understand that 'access' is not sufficient to have someone use or benefit from an innovation or solution. Much more needs to go into delivering this access with clear benefits.

Designing beyond the male default settings

We know that understanding the user is key to designing the right solution for that specific user group. Much of the world, whether it's medicine, physical infrastructure, or technology, has been built for the 'average' user, which has often meant men. Car companies are well known for testing crashes on dummies built to the specifications of male dummies. This means that women, or others with smaller body frames, are not protected in the same way as the average man. As a result, more women face injury risk as a result of crashes than men – in fact, women are 73 percent more likely than men to face injuries from crashes. [150] Smartphone sizes are often larger than what would be typically comfortable for a woman's hand size (~12cm width), making one-handed use difficult.[151] Most concerning, medical research and diagnostics build their evidence using male data: heart disease symptoms, drug trials, and treatment dosages. This results in potential misdiagnoses or outright exclusion of women from clinical recommendations.[152]

Needless to say, it is rather obvious that to reach the consumer segment you want to reach, you must start with a better understanding of that segment and not use a generic average that looks and behaves nothing like the target group.

Understanding the user means spending time in their environments, observing their behaviors, understanding how they work, and unlocking their pain points. Knowing that women spend far more of their day on care responsibilities is important before creating a solution that may require them to travel and incur transportation expenses to put money

---

[150] McMurray, Jeff, *Women face more injury risks in car crashes. So why are test dummies modeled after men?* (AP, June 23, 2025).
[151] Yee Huay, Goh, *From phones to face masks: Why some everyday products aren't designed for women* (CNA Lifestyle, September 10, 2021).
[152] Hamberg K., *Gender Bias in Medicine* (Women's Health, 2008).

into a digital wallet. Knowing that society may sanction women who interact with unknown males is important before investing in an extensive agent network that is mostly male.

Design that is iterative, with initial testing with the target user groups, is more likely to yield the outcomes desired rather than expanding services without initial testing. Developing strategies to address different types of user adoption journeys is also important. Not everyone is a first mover, and some user groups may take more time, experimentation, communication, and support than others.[153] And of course, nothing is ever truly final, and building feedback loops to continue to measure and adapt the solution is also essential.

Solving key pain points for customers

Research by CFI on micro and small firms in Lagos, Nigeria found that adoption of digital technology was greatly facilitated by simple and intuitive design. Interfaces that support multiple languages enabled more users to test and adopt an innovation. Another key feature of driving adoption was the reliability of the innovation. If users make a mistake or if the service drops on them midway, can they quickly recover from it? Are they able to get refunds and get support quickly? Of course, pricing is also a key variable. If technology is beyond their basic incomes, adoption will be difficult.

Low-cost transactions and minimal maintenance costs enable low-income users to not just test but also become regular users.

Technological innovation itself is not sufficient; users also need the technology to offer growth opportunities, whether that is access to financing to grow their firms or other ways to earn passive income.[154]

---

[153] Teppermen, Lawrence, *Why Great Technology Often Fails: Adoption Matters* (Medium, March 28, 2017).
[154] Totolo, Edoardo et al., *Small Firms, Big Impact* (CFI, April 2025).

One of the most successful digital innovations, M-Pesa in Kenya, was extremely successful because it met a clear and direct pain point that migrants had in Kenya. They needed ways to 'send money home' that didn't require them to get on a bus and spend days traveling back to their villages. M-Pesa now has over 42 million users, in a country with a population of 55 million, and has processed over 12 billion transactions.[155] As a result of its phenomenal growth trajectory, many mobile money deployments have tried to mirror M-Pesa's success. One that has perhaps succeeded is B-Kash in Bangladesh, which has 54 million accounts.[156]

Leverage social networks for adoption diffusion

In chapter 2, we discussed some of the emerging solutions that are helping service providers to address the digital divide. We discussed the use of 'edutainment' as a way to reach large numbers of users by depicting characters with whom they can relate and dealing with similar challenges in their lives. This type of intervention helps address multiple pain points for many low-income people – knowledge gaps, social and gender norms, and confidence or self-efficacy.

The Makutano Junction series in Kenya touches on information about opening a bank account. It also addresses the social norms around why a woman would want a separate bank account from her husband and demonstrates how communication with one's spouse can help address any misperceptions around the intent of having one's own account.

In many societies, a woman's desire to have her own account can be interpreted as a strategy to hide an illicit affair or a plan to leave her husband. In the show, the producers directly address this fear that men have that their wives may be doing something wrong, leveraging another important cultural reference by having the son encourage the father to be supportive of his wife. The show also brings in the role of peers in supporting the main character to try something out of her comfort zone,

---

[155] Bandura, Romina and Ramanujam, Sundar R., *Developing Inclusive Digital Payment Systems* (CSIS, September 21, 2021).
[156] Ifc.org

helping her to gain the confidence she needs to plunge into something she didn't think was for someone in her social class.

Social networks are a very important source of information and behavior monitoring in some societies. When a key influencer in society introduces something new – whether that's opening a bank account, getting a smartphone, or signing up to an e-commerce platform to sell her goods – then other women are more likely to follow. Leveraging social networks for technology adoption is an important tool that deserves significantly more attention.

An experiment in Malawi tested how information can be disseminated among farmers. Different methods were tested, distributing information to farmers who were in the right location, distributing information via government extension officers, and distributing information to 'networked' farmers, those who serve as role models or local champions. The experiment found that the farmers who were well networked were much more effective at the diffusion of their knowledge than others who obtained information for the experiment. The experiment concludes that adoption happens through a complex contagion process, where information should come from multiple sources before certain groups will be comfortable with its adoption.[157]

A study in India looked at adoption of piped water technology, based on social networks in the community.

They find that early adopters who are respected and trusted by other community members have a bigger impact on others' trust and take-up. Their status as trusted community member matters more than their wealth or demographics. This points to the importance of identifying the central individuals who can influence their networks for widespread uptake of technology in their communities.[158]

---

[157] Beaman, Lori et al., *Can Network Theory-Based Targeting Increase Technology Adoption?* (Yale University, 2018).
[158] Suzuki, Akiko et al., *The Effect of Social Network on Acceptability of New Technology in Developing Countries: A Case Study of Piped Water Adoption in Rural India* (Environment and Natural Resources Research, Vol. 8, No. 2., 2018).

Social networks in these contexts function as trust hubs, information conduits, and behavioral reinforcers—making them critical vehicles for spreading new technologies, especially where formal infrastructure or extension services may be limited.

Make it safe and reliable

Social networks can support diffusion of information that is both good for uptake and usage, or potentially detrimental if the information disseminated is about the bad experience they had or the scam that they couldn't get resolved. In 2023, I traveled and interviewed many rural residents in the northern Wetlands of Colombia. One of the recurring themes I encountered during this trip was the number of individuals who had been poorly served by the financial institutions in their region. One resident's identity was stolen, and a large loan was issued in their name to the scammer. The bank did nothing to help this person solve the identity theft problem and held them liable for the loan that was taken out by the scammers. One after the other, residents in this community relayed their own experiences or those of their networks, and it was clear that regaining trust would be a difficult task for any financial institution in that region.

Any provider that wants customers to speak well of its services must prioritize safety and reliability of their services and do their utmost to correct errors or scams when and if they happen. Otherwise, they risk knowledge diffusion theory working against them!

In chapter 9, we discuss consumer protection and market conduct issues that enable the safety and reliability of services. Safety is especially important for low-income users who do not have the cushion to incur losses.

Research with micro and small enterprises in five mega development cities – Addis Ababa, Delhi, Jakarta, Lagos, and Sao Paulo – shows that negative experiences with financial services abound.[159] The most

---

[159] CFI

common form of negative experiences is related to fraud and scams, as well as excessive fees or penalties.

Figure 1: Negative experiences with financial services in key LMIC cities

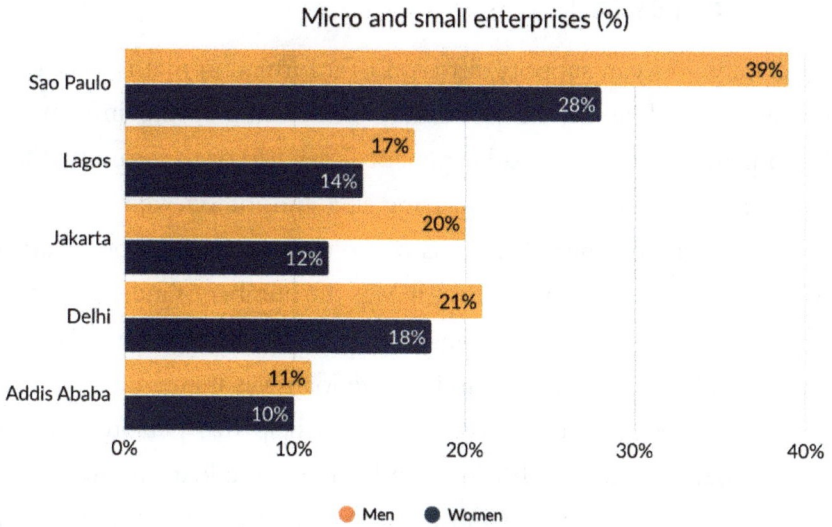

Micro and small enterprises (%)

City	Men	Women
Sao Paulo	39%	28%
Lagos	17%	14%
Jakarta	20%	12%
Delhi	21%	18%
Addis Ababa	11%	10%

● Men   ● Women

Source: CFI, Small Firms, Big Impact

Imagine you are a semi-literate vendor in Lagos, and you need to pay your supplier through mobile money. You enter the information on your phone, but then discover you made a mistake. You call the person to whom you inadvertently sent the funds, but they refuse to answer the phone. You contact the mobile money provider, and they either don't respond or state they can't do anything to help you.

Even more likely, you get on an endless loop of automated phone support where you can't reach a human being and none of the options address your needs. These kinds of experiences are very common, resulting in customers fearing the use of the service.

Customer recourse is one of the fastest and best ways to get trust and address the fear of using a service. What makes a recourse system effective? It takes four key elements: customers must know what the recourse system is; the system needs to be adapted and accessible to different user groups; resolutions need to be timely, and processes need to be predictable; and the system needs to engage users and be accountable to them.[160]

In Mexico, the Central Bank created a 24/7 hotline to address customer complaints and recourse. The system allows customers to communicate via multiple channels, including online chat, a chatbot, and the hotline. One of the leading banks in Mexico, BBVA, recognizing that older customers were struggling with long waiting times, introduced a priority service for older adults that shortened wait times to just five minutes. They also introduced support for digital authentication for older adults who were struggling with fingerprint scanning. A remote assistance team was able to cut the authentication time of older adults from three days to just nine minutes. These initiatives not only helped customers, but they also supported the bank's ability to reduce fraud and customer claims.[161]

Learn from what works

In the U.S., a FinTech called Current offers mobile banking services through partner banks. It has features that appeal to consumers such as early paycheck access, free overdraft, cryptocurrency support, and debit and credit cards. The FinTech is fully digital with no branches. In 2021, Current partnered with a famous YouTube influencer, MrBeast, to attract customers by offering a cash giveaway.

MrBeast announced the campaign on his social media, which received 18 million views in 24 hours. This created a massive surge in the Current app downloads and massive account sign-ups.[162] The focus of this campaign was to attract young customers, and the campaign helped create the 'cool' vibe that Current was aiming for. It targeted a social media influencer who was already reaching the user group they sought.

In Pakistan, Easypaisa, a Pakistani FinTech that offers a mobile wallet, launched a TikTok campaign targeting both rural and urban users. Easypaisa tested two forms of social media campaigns, the TikTok AI-

---

[160] BTCA, *Make recourse clear, quick and responsive* (BTCA, January 2024).
[161] ibid
[162] Banerjee, Agnishwar, *15 Best Fintech Marketing Campaigns That Set the Bar* (CleverTap, May 21, 2025).

powered Smart+ Campaigns versus traditional campaigns that are managed manually. The test used the same parameters for both approaches to ensure that the results could be attributable to the campaign method only. The Smart+ Campaign was able to convert significantly higher users than other mediums, while lowering its customer acquisition costs.[163]

In China, WeChat introduced gamification with a cultural twist to garner acceptance of its new product WeChat Pay. The company introduced something called e-Red Packets timed around the Lunar New Year. The e-Red Packets were created to be a virtual version of the red envelopes, which are traditionally used to gift money during the Lunar New Year. The Packets saw usage skyrocket, with 32 billion digital red packets exchanged in just six days.[164]

Concluding remarks

The examples in this chapter are meant to inspire and are not intended for direct replication. What is important to remember is that building a digital solution or infrastructure and expecting customers to just get it is a failing strategy.

Companies, governments, or others driving digital adoption must think about the specific user groups they are trying to reach and tailor their solutions and their diffusion strategies accordingly.

It starts with being clear about the target segment. It then requires understanding their needs, preferences and pain points. How one reaches a digital native teen will look very different than how one reaches rural women in Sub-Saharan Africa. While with some segments using social media influencers will succeed at incentivizing adoption, with others it will require understanding where this segment gets trusted information and equipping that source to serve as a champion for the product or service.

---

[163] Tiktok.com, EasyPaisa case study
[164] WeChat Chatterbox, *Red Packets – WeChat's Secret Weapon in Payments* (WeChat Blog, January 27, 2016).

Beyond the product or service, the experience needs to be safe and reliable. Users need to be able to test it without incurring losses of time or money. There are many companies and countries that have had remarkable success at reaching what seemed like unreachable segments. We can learn from them and take the time to iterate and adapt for the specific segment and community we are trying to serve.

Chapter 8

Limiting Digital Monopolies

We have a long history of monopolies

Throughout history, we have experienced the rise and fall of monopolies. One of the earliest documented stories is that of the East India Company. In 1600, it was granted a royal charter by Queen Elizabeth I of England. Its primary business was to trade with the East Indies, including present-day India, Indonesia, and surrounding regions. While initially, the East India Company faced competition from other European traders like the Portuguese and Dutch, it quickly dominated the seas and trade routes in the lucrative trade of spices, silk, cotton, tea, and indigo.

The company opened trading posts in various coastal locations and eventually dominated other trading companies, likely because it had access to financial resources that other smaller trading companies lacked. It was able to raise capital through the issuance of shares, allowing it to fund its voyages to the East Indies. Organized as a joint-stock company, it was able to pool resources among multiple investors. This structure allowed for sustained investment and long-term planning, providing stability and continuity in its operations.

Beyond its economic agility, the company also developed military capabilities and had a standing army and a naval fleet to protect its trading interests. This provided it with a further competitive advantage in conflicts and negotiations with other European companies.

Furthermore, the company formed strategic alliances and partnerships, sometimes playing rival factions against each other. By cultivating favorable relationships and securing favorable trade agreements, the company gained significant advantages over competitors.

Eventually, and after more than 170 years, the British government passed the Regulating Act of 1773, which increased its oversight over the company. But it was not until the Sepoy rebellion in India in 1857 that the company lost its control of India and was dissolved by the Crown in 1858. British Parliament passed the Government of India Act 1858, which transferred the powers and territories held by the East India Company to the British Crown, which assumed responsibility for governing India.

Modern-day monopolies use data

While it is hard to imagine a modern-day company with a standing army and navy, the powers of modern-day companies are flexed using more up-to-date warfare, namely data. An advisor to the Saudi Prime Minister, Dr. May Alobaidy, proclaimed data as the 'new oil, new gold of the digital era.'[165] Approximately 328.77 million terabytes of data are created each day.[166] What's a terabyte, you ask? It's 1,000 gigabytes. Needless to say, it's a lot.

Each time a person goes online to search Google, a data trail is created. Each time you purchase something using your credit card, either in a store or online, data trails are created. Each time you drive your car and use your E-Z Pass, a data trail is created. Every email, tweet, text message, Facebook or Instagram post, and the list goes on. Each day, Google processes 8.5 billion searches and WhatsApp users exchange 85 billion messages. Facebook has over 2 billion active daily users, and there are over 870 million tweets sent each day.[167]

---

[165] Alobaidy, Mai, *Data is the new oil, the New Gold of the Digital Era!* (LinkedIn, May 16, 2021).
[166] Duarte, Fabio, *Amount of Data Created Daily* (Exploding Topics, April 24, 2025).
[167] Rayaprolu , Aditya, *The State of Big Data in 2025: Key Insights and Developments* (Tech Jury, January 3, 2024).

The enormity of the role that data plays in the modern economy cannot be overstated. Beyond the searches, messages, and transactions themselves, there is a host of other 'data exhaust' that is a byproduct of each transaction. The cookies, the log files, the temporary internet files … all of these files are analyzed to study users' choices.

It might seem that the importance of data in the digital economy is a first-world issue. How can a poor person in a developing country have a data trail? The World Bank estimates that over 1.8 billion adults in developing countries are digitally included, that is, they have access to a phone. Of those, around 58 percent also have access to the internet.[168] Once someone is equipped with a phone and has internet access, the data trail begins. Data trails include:

- The frequency of someone topping up their phone
- The amount someone spends each time they top up their phone
- Number of calls someone makes and the duration of the calls
- Number of text messages
- Number of people in their social networks
- Which apps and how many are stored on their phone
- Their geolocation
- Use of mobile money, frequency of transactions, and size of transactions
- Funds entering their mobile wallets from government, friends, or work
- Value of their mobile wallet

---

[168] Fernandez, Maria and Salman, Arisha, *Global Landscape: Digital Trails of Digitally Included Poor People* (CGAP, April 2023).

These data points can be used to assess this individual, and this assessment is then used to determine whether this person is qualified for a government program, is credit-worthy to obtain a loan, has the profile of someone who is insurable, and a host of other decisions.

Data unlocks the potential for growth in the digital economy

The idea that someone's data trail can result in unlocking opportunities is appealing. This is especially the case for improving access to credit and removing the age-old requirement that someone needs collateral in order to borrow to start or grow a business. This has been the driving mantra of the inclusive FinTech space for quite some time.

Data is a unique resource, unlike any others such as oil, gold, or water. Some of its unique properties include:

- It is not a limited resource but can grow exponentially.

- It is generative. Data can create more data through its analysis.

- It is durable. It can't be depleted.

- It is non-rivalrous. One person's usage does not affect another person's ability to use the same data.

- It can be replicated, accessed, shared, and controlled remotely.

- Those controlling it can restrict access, but once it's shared, it can't be controlled.[169]

Converting these unique attributes to economic value is a clear opportunity for businesses. Many new companies have been enabled as a result of this incredible data resource.

---

[169] De La Chapelle, B. and L. Porciuncula, *We Need to Talk About Data: Framing the Debate Around Free Flow of Data and Data Sovereignty* (Internet and Jurisdiction Policy Network, 2021).

In developing countries, research by the Center for Financial Inclusion on inclusive FinTechs[170] has uncovered over 1,000 FinTechs as of 2022, many of which rely on data to build algorithms or to support decision making for identifying and serving customers.[171] The majority of the inclusive FinTech solutions offer credit, using algorithms to assess creditworthiness.

Data and network effects create formula for monopolistic behaviors in the digital economy

Most platform businesses use data and network effects to make money. The network effect is when there are benefits to using a product or service as more people are using it.[172] For example, people used to send faxes when there were fax machine on the other end to receive them. As fewer people use faxes, this technology has since declined. People purchase phones when their friends have phones. More recently, people join platforms such as Facebook, X, or WhatsApp when their friends do. There is no point in joining a platform if you are the only person in your network doing so.

The most well-known platform businesses are Meta, Apple, Microsoft, Alphabet, and Amazon, which are colloquially known as MAMAA. It's not hard to see how market share or monopolistic power is key to optimizing revenue in these business models. Once a company establishes its dominant market share, it's hard to imagine how smaller rivals can compete. Because these companies own the data that is generated on them as well as the network protocols that enable the data exchange, they use this data to create 'stickiness' thus making it hard for users to switch.

---

[170] See https://www.centerforfinancialinclusion.org/series/inclusive-fintech-50
[171] CFI, *Inclusive Fintech 50.*
[172] McIntosh, Daniel. *We Need to Talk About Data: How Digital Monopolies Arise and We Need to Talk About Data: How Digital Monopolies Arise and Why They Have Power and Influence Why They Have Power and Influence* (Journal of Technology, Law and Policy, Volume 23, Issue 2, January 2019).

Research on platform businesses reveals that there are 74 dominant digital platforms globally, and they are each valued at around $10 billion.[173]   MAMAA were able to generate $25 billion in profits in the first quarter of 2018 alone;[174] in 2025, first-quarter profits range between $16.5 billion for Meta to nearly $35 billion for Alphabet (Google).[175]

How can small firms compete?

Imagine a small firm in a developing country, say a neighborhood bodega selling food and household supplies. During the pandemic, customers were afraid to come to the shop, and there were government restrictions on gatherings and opening hours. Perhaps the business started to introduce delivery to survive, and it might have even gone online and joined one of the digital platforms that support small merchants with logistics, sourcing inventory, marketing and sales. Perhaps it was Jumia in Nigeria, MaxAB in Egypt, FlipKart in India, or Bukalapak in Indonesia.

Initially, the e-commerce platforms presented a compelling case to sidestep the pandemic restrictions and allow small businesses to be discoverable through a platform. The platforms also allowed small merchants to expand their reach well beyond their immediate communities. Over time, however, small businesses come to realize that competition on platforms is fierce. Now customers can see and compare products to thousands of other merchants selling the same things.

The most obvious example of the fate of small businesses on e-commerce platforms can be seen through the data and eyes of merchants on Amazon.

---

[173] Jin, Zhang and Yuxin, Yu, *The Monopoly and Governance of the Platform Economy in the Digital Era*, (Contemporary Social Sciences: No. 3, Article 8., 2021).
[174] McIntosh, Daniel. *We Need to Talk About Data: How Digital Monopolies Arise and We Need to Talk About Data: How Digital Monopolies Arise and Why They Have Power and Influence Why They Have Power and Influence* (Journal of Technology, Law and Policy, Volume 23, Issue 2, January 2019).
[175] The Times, *Google Owner beats forecasts and announces 70bn share buyback (The Times, April 24, 2025).*

Research by the Institute of Local Self Reliance[176] shows that as Amazon has grown, the number of small merchants in the U.S. has declined. Small retailers in the U.S. have fallen by around 40 percent in the 10 years between 2007 and 2017. As the total number has declined, Amazon's profits have continued to rise. Amazon's cut of revenue from sellers on its platform has continued to grow year on year, increasing from just 35 percent in 2016 to over 50 percent in 2022.

Figure 1: Amazon's cut of seller's revenue

Referral/Transactions, Fulfillment, Storage, Advertising and Other Fees

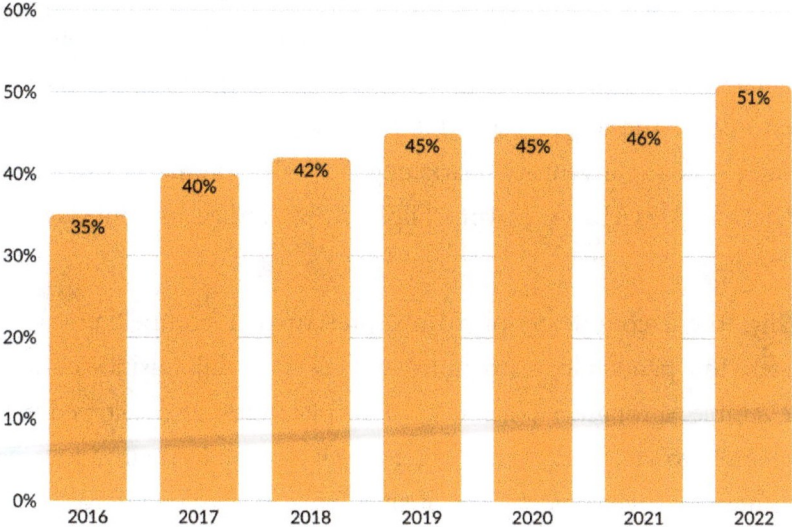

Source: Marketplace Pulse

Amazon is able to do this by serving as a gatekeeper to small merchants. Currently, around 50 percent of all online shopping in the U.S. is captured through Amazon. Through its algorithm, Amazon makes critical decisions about retailers. It intermediates the relationship with customers, thus creating a dependency on its platform and reducing the retailer's ability to grow market share without Amazon.

---

[176] Mitchell, Stacy and Know, Ron, *How Amazon Exploits and Undermines Small Businesses, and Why Breaking It Up Would Revive American Entrepreneurship* (Institute for Local Self Reliance, June 16, 2021).

As the largest platform, small retailers must use Amazon if they want to be visible at all; otherwise, they risk losing the massive market power that Amazon maintains as the biggest online marketplace in the world.

In developing countries, the platform economy is growing exponentially, and there is still fierce competition between platforms to attract merchants. In Indonesia, the e-commerce market has grown from $25 billion in 2019 to $73 billion in 2024.[177] There are four important e-commerce platforms: Shopee, Tokopedia, Bukalapak, and Lazada. Many of them are subsidizing merchants and offering add-on services to attract them and create stickiness. For Lazada, rather than taking large cuts of the merchant's revenue, it charges a small one-time fee for joining. Its revenue is generated from advertising and seller promotions.[178]

Figure 2: Top e-commerce platforms by market share in Indonesia (2022)

Platform	Market Share	Estimated Revenue
Shopee	36%	$18.7 billion
Tokopedia	35%	$18.2 billion
Bukalapak	10%	$5.2 billion
Lazada	10%	$5.2 billion

Source: Indonesia E-Commerce Sectors – Market Intelligence, U.S. International Trade Administration, U.S. Department of Commerce, 2022

Aware of the market dynamics in the U.S. and China, where large e-commerce monopolies have dominated the market, Indonesia has taken a more cautious regulatory approach. For example, it is studying closely the potential merger of Tik-Tok and Tokopedia, citing the risk of creating a monopoly. Tik-Tok, which is owned by China's Bytedance, offered to buy 75 percent share of Tokopedia for $840 million in January 2024.[179] The sale is still pending review by the Indonesian antitrust agency.

---

[177] Uzunoglu, Cihan, *eCommerce in Indonesia: Revenues Projected to Cross US$100 Billion in 2025* (ECDB, September 27, 2024).
[178] Business Times, *China goes for broke in Indonesian e-commerce* (Business Times, September 19, 2018).
[179] Reuters, *Indonesia antitrust agency finds risk of monopoly from TikTok's Tokopedia takeover,* (Reuters, May 29, 2025).

Despite the potential power imbalance, there is no question that the digital economy has been good for small merchants, at least for now. Research from the Center for Financial Inclusion in key developing cities – Addis Ababa, Lagos, Delhi, Jakarta, and Sao Paulo - shows that firms which adopted technology solutions, particularly digital payments, had greater labor productivity, increased business growth, and improved financial resilience. Striking the right balance between protecting consumers and merchants while facilitating platform growth will be crucial for any developing country.[180]

Beyond harm to merchants, monopolies reduce innovation and can erode worker protection

Over time, digital monopolies are potentially harmful to the small merchants who are aggregated through the platform and who have much less power to negotiate. Digital monopolies may also be harmful to other dimensions of society. The best example of this is China, where, until recently, the government has enabled a free hand for most of the digital platforms with minimal regulation. Researchers have noted that the evolution of the platform economy in China has begun to show cracks in that technological and scientific innovation are now seeing a slowdown.[181] China has two behemoth platforms – Tencent (internet and technology) and Alibaba (e-commerce) – which are in the global top 10. Other platform companies in China have also grown massively including JD.com (e-commerce), Didi (ride-hailing), Toutiao (news), and Meituan (e-commerce, services, travel, etc.). The scale of the digital economy is massive, representing nearly 35 percent of GDP as of 2019.

Digital monopolies can limit innovation by squeezing rivals even before they are a threat. Once a dominant player controls a market, we often see higher prices, lower quality customer service, and predatory behaviors like those seen from Amazon with its merchants.

---

[180] Totolo, Edoardo et al. *Small Firms, Big Impact* (CFI, April 2025)
[181] Jin, Zhang and Yu Yuxin, *The Monopoly and Governance of the Platform Economy in the Digital Era* (Contemporary Social Sciences, Number 3, Article 8, 2021).

Worker rights are another area where digital platforms have eroded standards around quality work. By treating workers as independent contractors, platforms have been able to evade standards around employment practices. In the U.S., platform work is now characterized "by poverty wages, hazardous conditions, job insecurity, a lack of bargaining rights, and a lack of access to unemployment or other safety net protections."[182] Countries such as Canada are enacting new rules focused on platform workers. Ontario passed a Digital Platform Workers' Rights Act in 2022, which, among other things, provides platform workers with minimum wages and rights against reprisals.[183] The European Parliament is also in the process of important discussions around the classification of workers and the rights to understand how algorithms are utilized to monitor and make decisions about their work.[184]

Reigning in digital monopolies is not straightforward

The traditional method of addressing monopolies is through antitrust regulation. Such regulation focuses on the interest of the consumers. However, the complexities of digital monopolies make traditional antitrust legislation insufficient, primarily as it excludes issues linked to data. Other important regulations on data protection are increasingly required.[185] Lina Khan, the former Chair of the Federal Trade Commission under Biden, is famous for her academic work on antitrust and competition policy, particularly for her famous article in the Yale Law Review "Amazon's Antitrust Paradox."

---

[182] Sherer, Jennifer and Margaret Polydock. *Flexible Work without Exploitation* (Economic Policy Institute, February 2023).
[183] Bader Law, *Digital Platform Workers' Rights Act: An Overview* (Bader Law, April 24, 2023).
[184] https://www.consilium.europa.eu/en/press/press-releases/2023/06/12/rights-for-platform-workers-council-agrees-its-position/
[185] McIntosh, Daniel, *We Need to Talk About Data: How Digital Monopolies Arise and Why They Have Power and Influence* (Journal of Technology Law & Policy: Vol. 23: Iss. 2, Article 2, 2019).

In this article[186] she states:

> *"This Note argues that the current framework in antitrust—specifically its pegging competition to "consumer welfare," defined as short-term price effects—is unequipped to capture the architecture of market power in the modern economy. We cannot cognize the potential harms to competition posed by Amazon's dominance if we measure competition primarily through price and output. Specifically, current doctrine underappreciates the risk of predatory pricing and how integration across distinct business lines may prove anticompetitive. These concerns are heightened in the context of online platforms for two reasons. First, the economics of platform markets create incentives for a company to pursue growth over profits, a strategy that investors have rewarded. Under these conditions, predatory pricing becomes highly rational—even as existing doctrine treats it as irrational and therefore implausible. Second, because online platforms serve as critical intermediaries, integrating across business lines positions these platforms to control the essential infrastructure on which their rivals depend. This dual role also enables a platform to exploit information collected on companies using its services to undermine them as competitors."*

In China, the exponential growth of the digital economy has led to considerable pushback by the government, including investigations of the two tech giants – Alibaba and Tencent. Since 2020, the government has strengthened the State Administration for Market Regulation (SAMR), providing it greater resources to pursue investigations and has given it greater flexibility to impose penalties and scrutinize mergers.[187] SAMR imposed more than 90 fines in 2021. In addition to antitrust legislation, China has also looked to regulate the internet more broadly, including cracking down on issues linked to cybersecurity and data privacy breaches.[188]

---

[186] Khan, Lina, *Amazon's Antitrust Paradox* (Yale Law Review, Vol 126, number 3, January 2017).
[187] Colino, Sandra Marco. *The Incursion of Antitrust into China's Platform Economy* (The Antitrust Bulletin 2022, Vol. 67(2) 237–258).
[188] Ibid

At the same time, China has also established its own program for monitoring the data created by the digital economy, known generally as its Social Credit System.[189] This system was created ostensibly to monitor and evaluate the trustworthiness of individuals, businesses and institutions, but it has raised concerns that it is being used as a surveillance tool for citizens.[190] Chinese authorities continue to tweak the program, but global observers continue to wonder how far the government will go in using this data and whether it risks turning into a ranking or blacklisting mechanism.

Europe has gone furthest and recently enacted the Digital Services Act and the Digital Markets Act. These acts provide a more updated view of 'gatekeepers' and aim to reduce the negative harm such players pose to the public and to the economy. Even the U.S., which is historically more pro-business and less likely to use regulations to stifle innovation, has stepped in to protect consumers' rights.

As mentioned earlier, Indonesia has taken a cautious approach, studying carefully the purchase of Tokopedia by TikTok. It also prohibited social media platforms like TikTok and WhatsApp to offer online shopping, blocking TikTok's initial foray into e-commerce when it launched TikTok Shop.[191]

---

[189] State Council, People's Republic of China (March 31, 2025).
[190] Donnelley, Drew, *China Social Credit System Explained – What is it & How Does it Work?* (Horizons, February 11, 2024).
[191] Reuters, *Indonesia antitrust agency finds risk of monopoly from TikTok's Tokopedia takeover* (Reuters, May 29, 2025).

Box 1: Reigning in monopolistic power in the U.S.

Legal actions against digital monopolies are becoming increasingly common as governments and regulatory bodies worldwide recognize the need for oversight. For instance, in 2020, the United States Department of Justice filed an antitrust lawsuit against Google, alleging that the company unlawfully maintained monopolies in search and search advertising markets. Similarly, the European Union has fined Google billions of euros across multiple cases for abusing its dominant market position in areas such as online shopping and Android operating systems. Additionally, Amazon faced scrutiny in 2021 when the Office of Fair Trading in the UK launched an investigation into its use of third-party seller data to bolster its product lines unfairly. In 2020, TikTok faced class action lawsuits for allegedly collecting users' data without consent, including biometric data. The lawsuits cited potential violations of Illinois' BIPA and the federal CFAA. In February 2021, TikTok settled these claims for $92 million, covering about 89 million U.S. users. [192] These lawsuits underscore the global concern over the unchecked power of digital platforms and their practices, prompting a necessary dialogue on the balance between innovation and regulation.

In Chapter 10, we will provide more insights on how competition policy, consumer protection and consumer awareness can help to address the imbalance of power between the tech players, consumers, and merchants.

---

[192] Allyn, Bobby, *Class-Action Lawsuit Claims TikTok Steals Kids' Data And Sends It To China* (NPR, August 4, 2020).

Chapter 9

Leveling the Playing Field

The cautionary tale of China

Chinese society was digitalizing rapidly through homegrown Internet giants: Alibaba for e-commerce, Tencent and WeChat for social networking and Baidu for Internet search. The rise of these tech giants was most often the result of regulatory nonchalance. At the time, the digitalization imperative was perceived as useful for Chinese economic growth and modernization. Government regulators saw the private sector boon in digitalization as aligned with their national interest. Until it wasn't.

In November 2020, billionaire founder of Alibaba Group, Jack Ma, disappeared for three months.[193] Alibaba, at that time a company with 800 million users, had expanded from its initial foray of e-commerce to become a tech giant in artificial intelligence and cloud computing. Ma had expanded his empire to include Ant Group, which facilitated digital payments through Alipay, a mobile finance app. The backbone of any e-commerce company is a reliable, trusted, and user-friendly digital payment solution. Other countries that have tried to expand ecommerce using cash on delivery or where there's no trusted digital payments platform have struggled to expand in the way that China's meteoric e-commerce growth has enjoyed.

---

[193] Peach, Sam, *Why did Alibaba's Jack Ma disappear for three months?* (BBC, March 20, 2021).

Ma's disappearance happened just before the Ant Group was going public on the Hong Kong and Shanghai stock exchanges. Ma was questioned by authorities, and then the IPO was suspended. Ma disappeared from public view for nearly three months after this.[194]

Alipay falls into what is otherwise termed a non-bank financial services firm. In China, these players are also often called the shadow banking system. Shadow banks offer many of the same services that regular banks do, like payments and credit, but don't offer savings services directly. What keeps them in the shadows is that they are not formally regulated by the central bank regulator in the country, which focuses its energy on deposit-taking institutions, which are more likely to create systemic risks should they fail.

China's non-bank players were growing at exponential rates between 2010 and 2020. Many proponents of inclusive finance were quick to support the rapid growth of the Chinese model, even admonishing the fact that the system had not reached sufficient numbers of the excluded.[195] Without cumbersome regulations, non-bank players can leverage data and take on risks that the traditional banking sector would find more difficult to emulate. These players, often relying on data and without legacy physical infrastructure, can operate more cheaply and can offer lower-cost loans without collateral and other traditional ways that banks secure credit.

The case of China is a cautionary one. While its GDP growth, poverty reduction, and digital economy are the envy of many countries, these upsides have been accompanied by many concerning outcomes.

Consequences of unfettered growth

Growth of the financial system using non-regulated players can have consequences. Typically, regulated financial institutions adhere to global standards set by Basel and other financial sector standard setters. Banks

---

[194] Au, Lavender, *Jack Ma Isn't Back* (Wired, June 15, 2023).
[195] Duflos, Eric and Ren, Li, *Financial Inclusion in China: Will Innovation Bridge the Gap?* (CGAP, April 21, 2014).

are required to have a minimum level of capital adequacy, liquidity coverage, capital buffers, and other measures to ensure banks are able to withstand losses should certain shocks affect the financial system.[196] Non-bank players are not required to adhere to similar standards and thus can cut corners and take on significantly higher risks. Furthermore, in many markets, these players can fall between the regulatory cracks, and there may not be one agency responsible for monitoring or capturing their effects on consumers, businesses, and the financial system at large. This is particularly true when lightly regulated players like payments providers move into loosely defined lending services. Few of us can forget the 2008-09 financial crisis in the U.S., which had global ramifications and was primarily a result of non-regulated financial institutions taking undue risks with sub-prime mortgages.

Stories of individuals losing their homes and wealth abound when financial markets are allowed to operate through shadow, unregulated players. Potential losses in China, as a result of shadow banking, is estimated to be significant. Bloomberg Economics estimates that 5 million people are potentially at risk of losing their jobs as a result of the downturn effects of bad debts in the housing sector in the country.[197] The financial crisis in the U.S. impacted 10 million households. In 2008, over 3 million households filed for foreclosures on their mortgages.[198]

Losses can be even more devastating in low- and middle-income economies where households have very little recourse or cushion. Research by the Carnegie Endowment for Peace found pervasive threats for low-income consumers and businesses in Africa due to poorly regulated and supervised financial intermediaries. Poor regulation and supervision are often a feeding ground for scammers and fraudsters.

---

[196] Basel Committee on Banking Supervision, *High-level summary of Basel III reforms* (Bank for International Settlements, April 2017).
[197] Bloomberg, *China's middle class battered by real-estate meltdown—and it might be just 'the beginning of more wealth losses'* (Fortune, December 17, 2023).
[198] *How the 2008 Housing Crash Affected the American Dream* (Investopedia, September 2021).

At a macro level, African countries are losing around $4 billion a year due to cyber-related risks. This can have a significant effect on GDP, estimated at a reduction of approximately 10 percent of GDP continent-wide.[199]

Table 1 provides an overview of common fraud, scams, social engineering, and other threats that people in Africa, as well as many other regions, face. Often, people who are most vulnerable to such threats are also the people who have the least capability, time, and resources to pre-empt or recover from such risks.

---

[199] *Anthony, Aubra, et al. Security and Trust in Africa's Digital Financial Inclusion Landscape, (Carnegie Endowment for Peace, March 2024.)*

Table 1: Examples of threats faced by consumers in weakly regulated digital finance markets

Types of threats	Definition
Social engineering	This type of threat involves some kind of scam that entices an unsuspecting user to reveal their personal data or spreading malware.
SIM swaps	This is when a scammer uses a second SIM to take control of a user's phone number. Through this, the scammer can reroute calls and text messages and possibly access someone's financial accounts.
Denial-of-service attacks (DDoS)	This type of attack floods a server, service or network with traffic overwhelming its ability to function.
False promotion fraud	In this scam, a user gets a promotion via a text message and they are encouraged to enter their PIN. The victim unwittingly provides access to the fraudster to access their account.
Ransomware and malware	This is a type of malicious software that blocks a user's ability to access their system. Typically, the scammer is seeking ransom to be paid to unblock the system.

Source: Anthony, Aubra, et al. Security and Trust in Africa's Digital Financial Inclusion Landscape, Carnegie Endowment for Peace, March 2024

Who sets the rules of the game?

Imagine a game where there are no rules. Who wins? Most likely, the most ruthless players who use whatever means, including force, to capture the spoils. A financial system with no rules would likely result in similar outcomes. As the rails of an economy, stability in the financial system goes hand in hand with stability in the economy. With the rise of the digital economy, fueled by digital payments and the monetization of data, balancing innovation with protection becomes the key role of policymakers and regulators.

By leveling the playing field, policymakers and regulators can enable new market entrants, reduce the power of incumbents, but also enable the little guy – whether that's an individual consumer or a small firm – to participate in the game. But how do policymakers and regulators do this when they have their own capacity limitations? And how do they guarantee that they are acting in the public interests, ensuring quality and customer choice and not unintentionally picking winners?

There is no simple answer to this conundrum. But there are important principles that policymakers and regulators need to uphold and examples from which they can learn.

Staying abreast of technological innovation

One of the most pressing challenges that policymakers and regulators face is actually staying abreast of how rapidly technology is changing how people shop, get information, learn, make decisions, or make payments. Perhaps nothing depicts this knowledge lag than observing the U.S. Congress interview the founders of the big technology firms like Meta or Google.

Some of the questions that have become comedic legends include:

- "How many data categories do you store?"

- "Are you willing to change your business model to protect individual privacy?"

- "How can Facebook remain free?"[200]

While Congress may not be as up to date as one would like, regulators in the U.S. and other G7 countries can invest resources to remain up to date. Many of these regulators collaborate, engage with the private sector directly, work with policy think tanks and academics, and collaborate on studies and reports on the latest issues.

---

[200] See https://www.youtube.com/watch?v=n2H8wx1aBiQ and https://www.youtube.com/watch?v=stXgn2iZAAY

For example, on the increasingly challenging issue of competition in the digital economy, G7 countries have collaborated on updating a compendium of approaches to regulating competition in the digital economy.[201]

Developing countries, on the other hand, face a much bigger knowledge lag and rely heavily on multilateral organizations, such as the World Bank, the Asian Development Bank, or the International Monetary Fund for knowledge on emerging technology and risks. While some developing country regulators are at the frontier of the technological revolution, like India and Kenya, many others are falling further behind. It is also becoming increasingly important for separate regulators within a country to share information and learnings with each other, as the previously distinct activities of banks, payments providers, and microfinance institutions are becoming increasingly interdependent and/or blurred, particularly with digitalization.

For these countries, ensuring that development organizations can support closing this knowledge gap is critical for addressing emerging risks, which are often no longer isolated in one jurisdiction but are increasingly global.

Enabling 'safe' innovation

As noted in Chapter 3, in recent years there has been a rapid rise in the number of regulatory sandboxes. These structures are essentially controlled experiments. A regulator allows a private player to test their solution on a small set of willing consumers to observe how the innovation works and to assess any potential risks to users. Through dialogue with the private sector players, the regulator and the providers can work together to tweak the innovation to ensure minimal collateral damage or harm. As of 2020, the World Bank had tracked 73 FinTech sandboxes in 57 countries.[202]

---

[201] Compendium of approaches to improving competition in the digital economy. November 2023.
[202] Appaya, Sharmista and Haji, Mahjabeen, *Four years and counting: What we've learned from regulatory sandboxes* (World Bank Blogs, November 18, 2020).

Perhaps the most well-known regulator for safe innovation is the Financial Conduct Authority (FCA) of the UK. It is the first country that established a sandbox, and many countries have emulated its design. The FCA has supported 160 businesses to test their products, and it has authorized 90 per cent of these solutions.[203] Some of the noteworthy alumni of the FCA's sandbox are in table 2 below.

Table 2: Examples of alumni of the FCA's regulatory sandbox

Company	Description of Offering
Mortgage Kart *Mortgagekart.com*	This is a digital solution that offers customers automated advice on mortgages.
Mettle *Mettle.co.uk*	This solution focuses on small business owners, especially solo entrepreneurs, and offers them a current account. It also helps them with smart invoicing and easy receipts and manages their entire payment cycle.
Pluto *Meetpluto.io*	This solution works on Facebook Messenger and enables customers to buy and manage travel insurance via a chatbot. Customers can ask the chatbot questions about coverage. It also handles claims.

Source: https://www.fca.org.uk/news/press-releases/fca-reveals-fourth-round-successful-firms-its-regulatory-sandbox

Clarifying accountability

The United States has a myriad of regulatory bodies that oversee different financial institutions. The Federal Reserve, the Federal Deposit Insurance Corporation (FDIC), the Office of Comptroller of the Currency, and the Securities and Exchange Commission (SEC) are just some of the regulatory bodies that oversee financial firms.

While the U.S. system may be one of the most complex in the world, it is nonetheless a common reality that firms operating in the financial system may be overseen by one or more regulatory bodies.

---

[203] Pritchard, Sarah, Speech entitled *How regulation can prepare the ground for economic growth* (Financial Conduct Authority, September 27, 2022).

Banks are perhaps the most straightforward entities with clearly demarcated regulators. Non-bank players, like leasing companies, may also have a clear regulator. Insurance providers will have their own regulator. And, then some of the new innovators may fall outside of these regulatory bodies altogether. PayPal, for example, is not under the jurisdiction of the Federal Reserve system. It is licensed as a money transmitter by different states.[204]

Firms entering these complex regulatory environments are challenged to understand to whom they report. The regulatory compliance costs can be staggering, especially for new start-ups. Simplifying the regulatory landscape can go a long way in helping to ensure that innovations have clear oversight by the right agencies and don't fall between the cracks. This often requires regulators to engage directly with one another within and across countries.

The Reserve Bank of India (RBI) has stayed abreast of market innovations by meeting with emerging FinTech firms regularly and collaborating with other regulatory bodies, particularly the Ministry of Finance, to ensure there is sufficient market conduct supervision. This structured approach serves two functions – it allows it to stay up to date on developments in the market and also ensures that new entrants have information on their compliance and regulatory requirements.[205]

Promoting competition

As noted in Chapter 8, firms in the digital economy benefit from network effects and data, which can create high concentration in one or a handful of large firms. This tendency toward monopolistic power can have adverse effects for consumers and may create scenarios where firms are 'too big to fail', whereby regulators step in to subsidize these firms rather than let them fail. Competition policy in the digital economy is challenging because the traditional rules for determining harm to consumers – high prices – may not be the single issue that is created by

[204] https://www.paypal.com/us/webapps/mpp/licenses
[205] Kalra, Jaspreet, *India regulator bolsters scrutiny of fintechs with more inspections* (Reuters, February 21, 2024).

monopolistic power. Thus, regulators have to redefine what new measures they need to better understand harms to consumers.

An important example of how competition in the digital age can look differently than in the analog economy is the case of the Apple phone. Apple has created an ecosystem where developers, payment apps, messaging services, and a variety of other ancillary services on the phone are smooth for Apple users but have significant friction for non-Apple users. This creates a situation where consumers must stay within the Apple ecosystem to have a smooth experience, not necessarily because these services are what they prefer. By creating a major hurdle for other developers, Apple is building a moat around its products. As of this writing, the Justice Department was suing Apple for what they term as 'exclusionary conduct,' which reinforces this moat and makes it difficult for individuals to switch to cheaper phones. The Justice Department is stating that this creates additional burdens to society affecting consumers, developers, and businesses.[206]

In developing countries, many international technology firms can invest enormous resources and immediately squash home-grown solutions. While in some countries, particularly large developing countries like Indonesia or India, local players can maintain a competitive advantage, this is often a result of restrictive regulations.

Smaller countries may not have the same regulatory heft nor the home-grown innovation capacity to compete with these global players. We have seen Uber buy many regional ride-hailing companies: it purchased Careem, which was native to the Middle East region; it invested in Jump, a bike-sharing platform operating in the U.S. and Eastern Europe;[207] and now it owns a significant share of Grab, which operates in Singapore and Indonesia.[208]

---

[206] Department of Justice, Press release entitled *Justice Department Sues Apple for Monopolizing Smartphone Markets* (DOJ, March 21, 2024).
[207] Dickey, Megan Rose, *Uber acquires bike-share startup JUMP* (TechCrunch, April 9, 2018).
[208] Britzky, Haley, *Uber to buy stake in Southeast Asian rival Grab* (Axios, March 25, 2018).

Equipping consumers and firms with capacity and skills

Up until now, the conversation has been about how policymakers and regulators can influence the innovations that providers put out in the market. This can already go a long way in creating a safe and secure digital economy. There will always be the early adopters who will jump in and try any new digital solution. These early adopters may be able to take risks and perhaps can afford to make mistakes. The vast majority of people in developing countries may not be able to take the same risks with their personal security and funds.

To avoid the inevitable fraud, scams, or other vulnerabilities, support of innovation must go hand in hand with equipping individuals and small firms with the knowledge to make informed decisions and the ability to recover losses should they make a mistake or experience harms. Too often, countries think that improving digital literacy means offering classroom training. But significant evidence shows that this form of capacity development does not result in the kind of outcomes that are commensurate with the investment.

Increasingly, evidence supports embedding learning opportunities and sufficient safety measures inside digital solutions so that consumers can learn by doing, without the fear of making a mistake. In addition to these embedded design solutions, ensuring consumer recourse is critical.

That is, a consumer who makes a mistake must be able to recover their losses in a way that they understand, and without creating additional loss of time and resources.

Estonia is one of the economies that has taken meaningful steps to reduce harms to consumers and firms through a myriad of embedded protection measures into their digital economy design. The country established the Information Technology Foundation for Education (HITSA) as a non-profit association, working alongside notable universities and private actors in the country including the University of Tartu, the Tallinn University of Technology, Eesti Telekom and the ITL.

The Foundation's mandate is to embed digital skills in all levels of the education system in Estonia. It also focuses on teaching methods to ensure that those also utilize the latest technology and digital skills.

Additionally, the government of Estonia created the Computer Emergency Response Team of Estonia (CERT Estonia) in 2006, which manages security throughout the digital economy, dealing with and managing security incidents, once these are flagged by consumers or firms. CERT also focuses on preventative security through digital public governance measures.[209]

Ensuring a feedback loop on consumer experience

How does a regulator know that an innovation is working? While usage numbers tell you something about adoption, they don't say enough about the quality of the experience. Regulators need real-time information on frictions that consumers are experiencing as they are using new digital solutions.

In digital finance, some regulators are collecting consumer complaints directly. For example, the Philippines Central Bank, Bangko Sentral ng Pilipinas, invested in a ChatBot called BOB (BSP Online Buddy) that collects customer complaints.

Customers can send messages by SMS, via Facebook Messenger, or directly on the Central Bank's Facebook page. The ChatBot uses AI and natural language processing and communicates in English, Filipino, and Taglish.[210] Other countries are following this lead, including Ghana, Cote D'Ivoire, and Rwanda.[211]

Other jurisdictions are scraping data on social media and analyzing it as an alternative source of information on potential consumer risks and

---

[209] Interoperable, *Estonia 2024: Digital Public Administration Factsheet* (Interoperable, July 2024).

[210] De Vera-Yap, Charina B., *A Chatbot Named BOB and Other Consumer Protection Measures in the Philippines* (FinDev Gateway, July 6, 2023).

[211] Cambridge SupTech Lab, *Case Study: Financial consumer protection suite with next-generation, AI-powered, chatbot supported complaints management* (Cambridge University, December 2024).

scams.[212] The Financial Conduct Authority (FCA) in the UK uses a 'digital listening tool' that scans social media, blogs, chat forums, and websites to identify consumer complaints and potential scams. It has focused especially on how financial firms market their products online.[213] One area where the FCA has taken action is around the promotion of cryptocurrencies to UK residents.[214] In 2024, it blocked more than 10,000 misleading financial promotions on Facebook, Instagram, and YouTube.[215] It has warned of the rise of financial influencers who provide investing advice without proper qualifications or certifications. FCA's actions have led to some social media platforms limiting advertising to only registered financial institutions.

Some regulators are testing consumer advisory boards.[216] The U.S.'s Consumer Financial Protection Bureau (CFPB), established under the Obama administration, created the Consumer Advisory Board (CAB). It is a formal advisory body which advises the CFPB on topical consumer issues such as fair lending and FinTech innovations.

The makeup of the board is representative of community groups, experts on consumer protection, representatives of historically marginalized communities, and experts on financial sector innovations. The body operates transparently with meeting agendas and minutes made publicly available.[217]

South Africa, through the Financial Sector Conduct Authority (FSCA) chose a similar model, launching its own Financial Services Consumer Panel in 2023. The panel offers structured consumer insights and identifies emerging risks within financial services.[218]

---

[212] Tully, Melissa and Madrid-Morales, David, *Measurement of Consumer Protection Complaints on Social Media* (Innovations for Poverty Action, April 2021).
[213] McMillan, Paul, *Chris Jackson: How will the FCA monitor social media?* (MoneyMarketing, April 3, 2013).
[214] Financial Conduct Authority, *Financial promotions data 2024* (FCA, February 7, 2025).
[215] Sweney, Mark and Jolly, Jasper, *Scams: FCA blocks more than 10,000 ads from Instagram, Facebook and YouTube* (The Guardian, February 3, 2023).
[216] Consumer Financial Protection Bureau, *Consumer Advisory Board.*
[217] ibid
[218] CGAP, *Tool 9: Consumer Advisory Panels* (CGAP, June 2023).

Increasingly, policymakers and regulators rely on civil society organizations to provide consumer-facing information that they may not have the resources or bandwidth to collect themselves. In Chapter 11, we'll cover these actors in greater depth. One of the emerging players shedding light on the experiences of consumers with digital finance is Consumer International's Fair Finance initiative. Its 2023 report covering a sample of 25 economies at different levels of consumer protection (developed, transitioning and emerging),[219] shows that there is progress toward addressing consumer needs, offering fairer, safer, and a more level playing field, but there's still much work to be done.

Figure 1: Fair digital finance index scores 2022 versus 2023

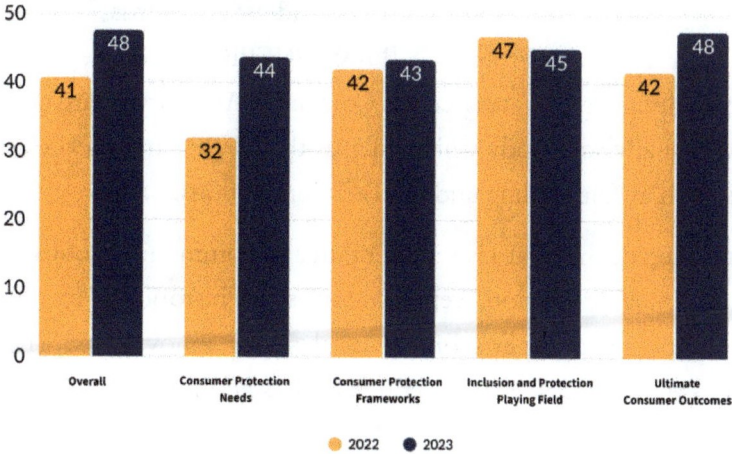

Source: *Consumer International's Fair Finance initiative*

While the digital economy promises a decentralized utopia or democratization of knowledge and decision making, the reality is far from this. The role of policy making and regulation is only heightened in this new digital world where there is constant change and iterations of products, where the risks are proliferating and ever-changing, and where firms and individuals do not have the time or resources to stay abreast of how to protect themselves. Fortunately, many policymakers and

---

[219] Developed (Malaysia, India, Uganda, Ecuador, and St. Lucia), transitioning (Fiji, Indonesia, Russia, Bangladesh, Kenya, Nigeria and Ivory Coast) and emerging (Myanmar, Tajikistan, Costa Rica, Mexico, Sudan, Lebanon, Pakistan, Nepal, Mali, Niger, Rwanda, Zimbabwe, Tanzania).

regulators recognize they are playing a game of catch-up and are rightly investing in leveling the playing field. For developing countries, policymakers and regulators cannot do this on their own and must rely on the support of development actors to support their capacity. We turn to this in Chapter 10.

Chapter 10

Development Cooperation

The backdrop is bleak for developing countries

The IMF reports that government debt has increased substantially in the past decades. This phenomenon is not limited to developing countries but also extends to developed countries. The rise in expenses due to COVID-19 was one of the accelerants, as are rising interest rates, energy costs, inflation, and food. Public debt is expected to exceed GDP in advanced economies by 2028 and reach 80 percent in developing economies.[220]

Against this backdrop, new global challenges are emerging. Food security, geopolitical shifts, trade disruptions, regional wars, continued risks of pandemics, and a host of localized challenges like climate-related floods,[221] fires,[222] locust infections,[223] and extreme heat limiting certain workers.[224] Needless to say, governments are overextended, both financially and with regard to human capacity.

---

[220] Adrian, Tobias, Gaspar, Vitor and Gourinchas, Pierre-Olivier, *The Fiscal and Financial Risks of a High-Debt, Slow-Growth World* (IMF Blog, March 28, 2024).
[221] Davies, Richar, *Europe – Storms Trigger Flash Floods in Poland, Czechia, Germany and Italy* (Floodlist, June 25, 2021).
[222] European Space Agency, *Counting wildfires across the globe* (ESA, August 3, 2023).
[223] Ogema, Nelson Mandela and Broom, Fiona, *Famine risk for millions in second locust wave* (PhysOrg, May 28, 2020).
[224] Shivji , Salimah, *India's outdoor labourers struggle to cope as country faces new reality of extreme heat waves* (CBC, May 21, 2023).

With governments stretched, what does this mean for their ability to invest in and benefit from the digital economy? The recent rise in the digital divide tells us something about the tradeoffs developing countries are making. Figures 1 and 2 provide a snapshot of internet access at home for every region of the world, looking at both urban and rural areas. There are huge variances between urban and rural areas globally, with nearly twice as many urban households with internet as rural households.

Looking at the data by GDP (Figure 1), we see that Least Developed Countries (LDCs) are three times less likely to have internet in urban households than in developed economies. Land Locked Developing Countries (LLDCs) fare slightly better than LDCs, but only in urban areas.

Figure 1: Households with computer and/or internet access at home
Regoions of the world 2019

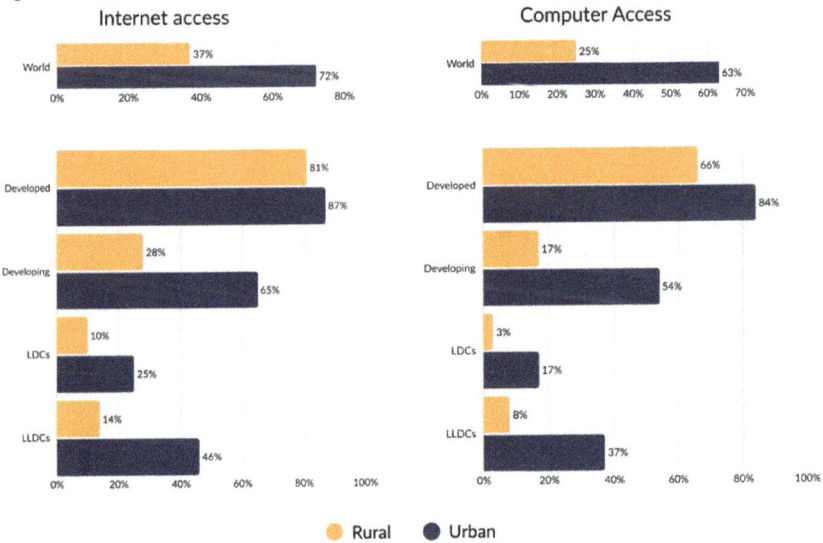

Internet access

	Rural	Urban
World	37%	72%
Developed	81%	87%
Developing	28%	65%
LDCs	10%	25%
LLDCs	14%	46%

Computer Access

	Rural	Urban
World	25%	63%
Developed	66%	84%
Developing	17%	54%
LDCs	3%	17%
LLDCs	8%	37%

● Rural ● Urban

Source: Internet Society

In every region of the world, there are major gaps between urban and rural households, except for Europe, where the gap is less than 10 percentage points. The Americas, Asia & the Pacific, and the Arab States are all regions with substantial gaps between urban and rural areas with regard to internet access.

Figure 2: Households with computer and/or internet access at home, *Regions of the world 2019*

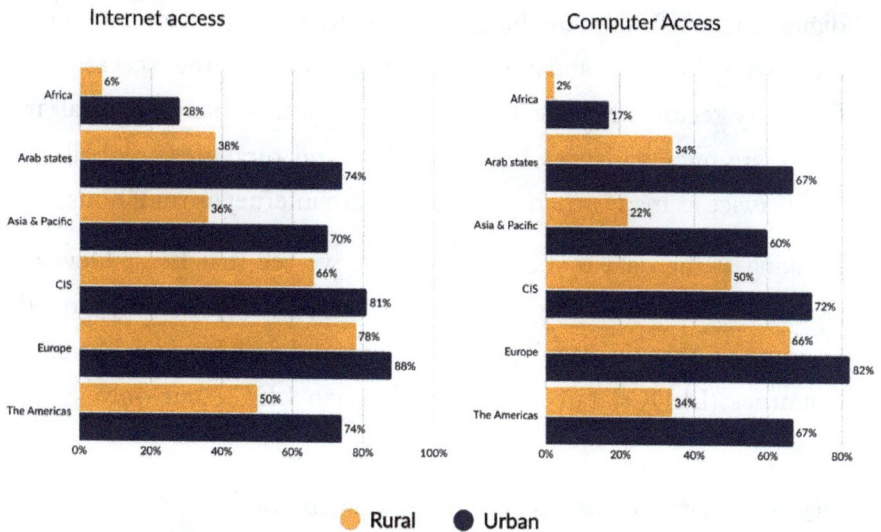

Internet access

Region	Rural	Urban
Africa	6%	28%
Arab states	38%	74%
Asia & Pacific	36%	70%
CIS	66%	81%
Europe	78%	88%
The Americas	50%	74%

(scale: 0% 20% 40% 60% 80% 100%)

Computer Access

Region	Rural	Urban
Africa	2%	17%
Arab states	34%	67%
Asia & Pacific	22%	60%
CIS	50%	72%
Europe	66%	82%
The Americas	34%	67%

(scale: 0% 20% 40% 60% 80%)

● Rural   ● Urban

Source: Internet Society

As we noted in Chapter 2, when using a gender lens, the digital divide is just as concerning. In LDCs, the gender digital divide has actually grown between 2013 and 2017 and is now close to 30 percentage points. This compares to a stagnant 15 percentage points in developed countries. Regionally, Africa has the largest gender digital divide, also growing between 2013 and 2017. Only in Europe is the gender digital divide negligible.

Figure 3: Gender digital divide across regions

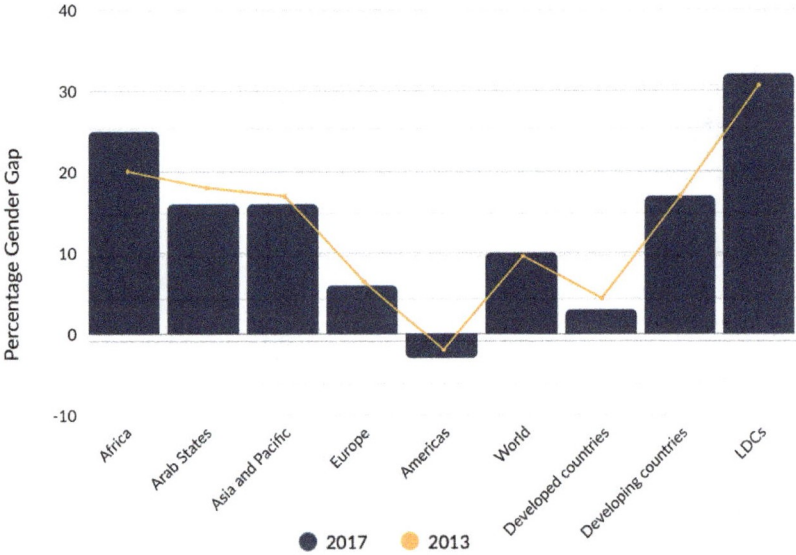

Source: OECD, Bridging the Digital Divide

There is no shortage of policy documents, manifestos, how-to guides, and calls to action about what governments should do to take advantage of the digital revolution. Box 1 is the digital manifesto developed by the Pathways for Prosperity Commission in the UK for developing countries to get ahead in the digital age.[225] But given their fiscal constraints and the sheer number of competing priorities, how can developing countries prioritize digital development?

[225] Pathways for Prosperity Commission, *Building on the work of the Pathways for Prosperity Commission* (Oxford). https://pathwayscommission.bsg.ox.ac.uk/

Box 1: Digital manifesto: How developing countries can get ahead in the digital age

1. Design a country-wide holistic digital strategy
2. Empower citizens for the digital age
3. Secure Citizens' data
4. Provide a social safety net
5. Build foundational digital systems
6. Nurture and enabling investment environment
7. End digital exclusion
8. Transform the health and education of your population
9. Create adaptive localized tech regulation
10. Coordinate internationally

Source: Pathways for Prosperity Commission in the UK

Can development donors come to the rescue?

Despite rising indebtedness across the globe, official development assistance (ODA) as measured by the Organization for Economic Co-operation and Development (OECD) for the Development Assistance Committee (DAC) members[226] was at an all-time high, rising to $211 billion in 2022, representing a 17 percent increase in real terms over 2021.[227] That was the fourth consecutive year that ODA reached an all-time high. Much of the increase can be explained by spending on the Ukraine crisis (see Figure 4 below), both in terms of humanitarian funding to Ukraine but also domestic costs that European donors have invested in hosting and providing social services to refugees in their countries.

---

[226] Australia, Austria, Belgium, Canada, Denmark, the European Union, Finland, France, Germany, Greece, Ireland, Italy, Japan, South Korea, Luxembourg, the Netherlands, New Zealand, Norway, Portugal, Spain, Sweden, Switzerland, the United Kingdom, and the United States
[227] OECD DAC at https://www.oecd.org/dac/financing-sustainable-development/development-finance-standards/official-development-assistance.htm

Figure 4: Historical official development assistance

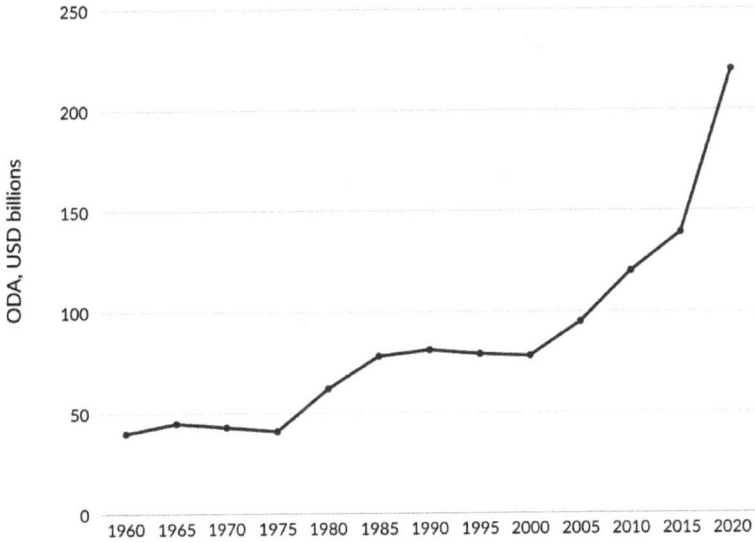

With the rise in conservative governments in many parts of the world, and the election of President Donald Trump in the U.S., the ODA picture is changing fast. Historically, the largest donor in the world, representing 40 percent of all ODA, United States Agency for International Development's (USAID) closure is having significant ripple effects everywhere, including in the U.S. itself where many contractors and non-profit agencies have had to close down or dismiss hundreds of their staff. The USAID closure itself has left thousands of government workers unemployed. The full extent of what this closure will mean for developing countries is still unfolding. Early signs point to significant harms for the most vulnerable segments of society, such as refugees and those living with HIV, as the U.S. government was one of the leading donors in these areas. Estimates by the African Center for Disease Control indicate at least two to four million additional Africans are expected to die as a result of the USAID cuts.[228]

---

[228] Cullinan, Kerry, *Africa CDC: Aid Cuts Will Result in Millions More African Deaths* (Health Policy Watch, March 20, 2025).

135

But more than just USAID, many European funders have also flagged future declines in ODA as they shift their attention to their own security concerns, given the Trump administration's reluctance to uphold its historic security relationships. In 2024, France cut €742 million from its ODA budget, representing a 12.5 percent reduction.[229] Germany announced a €2 billion reduction in its aid budget for 2024.[230] The Dutch government plans to reduce development aid by €300 million in 2025, followed by more significant cuts in 2026 and 2027.[231]

It is hard to imagine that development donors will be able to extend significant assistance to help developing countries prioritize digital development, let alone more pressing emergencies like natural disasters and other humanitarian needs. While it is impossible to predict whether the rightward shift in politics will persist in the long-term, it is nonetheless clear that Europe will likely continue to prioritize its own security given broader geopolitical shifts and the decline in U.S. power and willingness to maintain its global security role. Even beyond a Republican U.S. administration, relying on the United States is no longer something that many European or Asian countries can do in the future and realignment of political alliances is in motion as of this writing.

In this new world order, self-reliance becomes the foremost strategy that most developing countries need to prioritize. And the focus for the existing development funding is to ensure it is catalytic and not just plugging holes but supporting governments to solve their own challenges using domestic resources.

---

[229] Focus2030, *France reneges on its official development assistance* (Focus2030, April 30, 2025).
[230] Gulrajani, Nilima and Pudussery, Jessica, *With the knives out on development spending, have we reached 'peak aid'?* (The Guardian, January 23, 2025).
[231] Government of the Netherlands, *Budget Day 2024: lower cutbacks to embassies; major retrenchment on development aid* (Government of the Netherlands, September 18, 2024).

What are the biggest shifts in development cooperation?

The current political climate and rising security and migration concerns have shifted the priorities of many development donors.

First, many European countries aim to reduce the refugee influx. The fear of a flood of refugees from North Africa and the 'neighborhood' explains a significant amount of the attention European donors have given to initiatives that entice people to stay where they are. One of the most visible of these initiatives is the EU's agreement with Turkey called the Facility for Refugees in Turkey. In essence, the EU funds Turkey for hosting and keeping refugees on its soil to reduce their march westward. The program commenced in 2011 and has since disbursed more than €11 billion.[232] Other initiatives have tried to influence policy reform in some refugee-hosting countries to enable refugees to get employment in their host countries, again with the premise that if employed, they are less likely to travel to Europe. In Jordan, for example, the EU signed a trade agreement that would give Jordan preferential trade provided it created 200,000 jobs for Syrian refugees.[233]

Second, donors are increasingly spending development funds domestically, classified as in-donor spending on refugees. In-donor spending is estimated at $31 billion out of the total $211 billion reported in 2022, making up a full 13 percent of ODA that year.[234] Figure 5 below shows the two significant spikes in the in-donor refugee costs, roughly aligning with the Syrian and Ukrainian refugees' crises.

---

[232] European Commission, *The EU continues to provide much needed assistance to refugees and host communities in Türkiye* (EC, September 27, 2023).
[233] Sarrado, Olga and Dunmore, Charlie, *New deal on work permits helps Syrian refugees in Jordan* (UNHCR, October 13, 2017).
[234] OECD

Figure 5: In-donor refugee costs reported as ODA (1992-2022)

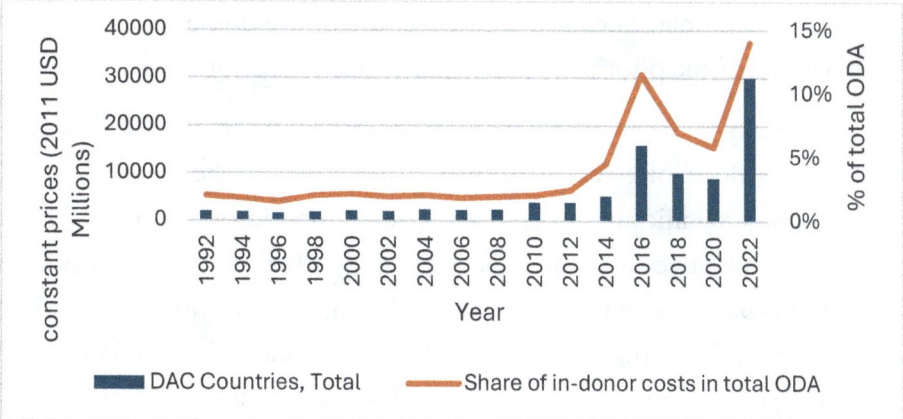

Source: OECD

Third, there is a new crop of international players vying for geopolitical influence by becoming donors themselves. Perhaps no country stands out as vividly as China, but Turkey, India, and many Arab donors are also significant actors in the development mix today. While China is not an official DAC member, it does provide data to the OECD voluntarily, as do a host of other emerging donors. China's estimated foreign assistance went as high as US$6.8 billion in 2018 but was estimated to decrease thereafter due to domestic and COVID-related expenditures.[235] As a percentage of Gross National Income (GNI), Turkey, Saudi Arabia, Qatar, and the UAE are now significant players, outside of the traditional DAC set of countries, according to the OECD. While these new crops of donors are important in their own right, they are not full replacements for the U.S. or European donors given that their priorities are different, mostly focusing on securing raw materials, food production or their energy needs. We are thus not likely to see a focus on the most vulnerable countries or sectors like global health, which have historically received the bulk of development funding.

---

[235] Kitano, Naohiro and Miyabayashi, Yumiko, *Estimating China's Foreign Aid: 2019-2020 Preliminary Figures* (JICA, December 14, 2020).

Figure 6: Top donors – other bilateral players outside of DAC

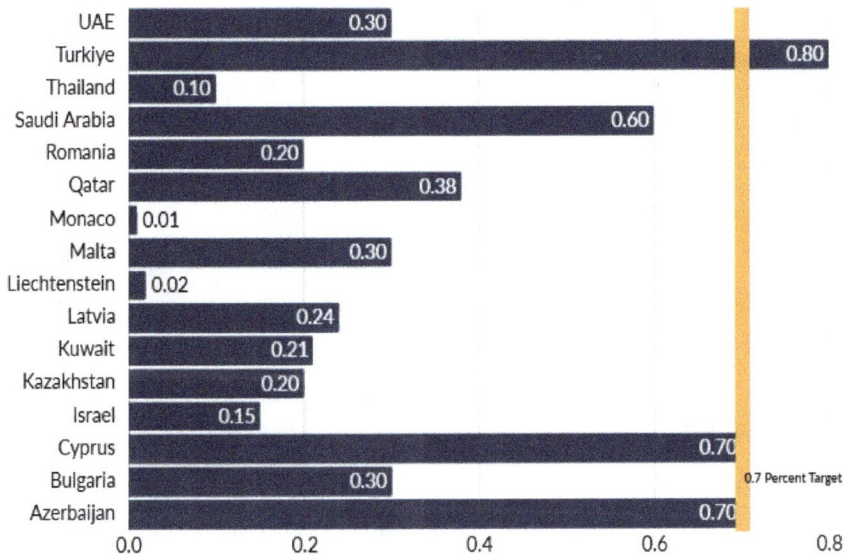

Country	Value
UAE	0.30
Turkiye	0.80
Thailand	0.10
Saudi Arabia	0.60
Romania	0.20
Qatar	0.38
Monaco	0.01
Malta	0.30
Liechtenstein	0.02
Latvia	0.24
Kuwait	0.21
Kazakhstan	0.20
Israel	0.15
Cyprus	0.70
Bulgaria	0.30
Azerbaijan	0.70

0.7 Percent Target

Source: Flourish

Fourth, a focus on 'returnable capital' or 'blended finance' is giving donors a way to shift the discourse domestically by making ODA an investment and leveraging the private sector. This shift has both positive and negative consequences. On the one hand, it does speak to in-donor political priorities, and it does subsidize the risks that private sector actors may perceive when investing in developing countries. According to Convergence, a blended finance data hub, blended structures have mobilized US$123 billion since the inception of reporting in 2014.[236] Blended structures can unlock private capital that may have otherwise not been able to absorb the risks of certain development-oriented investments. On the other hand, shifting limited grant funding into investable structures means that fundamental issues that rely on public subsidy, like government capacity, policy support, or public infrastructure, are de-emphasized. This is particularly troubling as these are precisely what is needed to support economies in the digital revolution.

---

[236] https://www.convergence.finance/blended-finance

To address this risk, donors need to be intentional and catalytic in how they invest their limited subsidies to ensure that they are leveraging and contributing to policy reform, core infrastructure and capacity constraints that would unlock private, commercial resources.

Fifth, philanthropic funding complements ODA, but does not replace it. In 2025, and since the closure of USAID, many philanthropic donors have announced significant increases in their giving. The most significant was the Gates Foundation's announcement that it would double its giving and spend down its endowment within 25 years. Bloomberg Philanthropies has announced a pledge to cover the U.S. commitment to the UN Framework Convention on Climate Change. Their funding for climate in 2023 accounted for $4.8 billion.[237] MacArthur announced it would increase its payout from the mandatory 5 percent of its endowment to 6 percent, which amounts to an additional $150 million of giving a year.[238] However, there are political pressures against many philanthropic donors that are perceived to be 'woke' and are being targeted by the Trump administration with potential for increased taxation on their endowments and even loss of their foundation status. These political pressures have resulted in relatively few foundations taking public positions to increase their outlays to avoid being targeted by the Trump administration.[239]

Despite these important announcements, philanthropic funding for development purposes is estimated at 1/3 of the volumes of ODA.[240] Philanthropic funding cannot fill the gap that is being created by these significant shifts in ODA funding priorities. In fact, given its vulnerabilities to the same political shifts, philanthropic funding is as much at risk as development cooperation itself.

---

[237] Gawel, Anna, *A hard look at the mass termination of USAID awards* (Devex Newswire, February 28, 2025).
[238] Beaty, Thalia, *MacArthur Foundation to increase giving for two years in response to 'crisis'* (AP, February 27, 2025).
[239] Callahan, David, *Inside Philanthropy Toplines (Inside Philanthropy, May 23, 2025).*
[240] Interaction

Bill Gates doubles giving to $200 billion, says philanthropists can't cover government cuts

PUBLISHED THU, MAY 8 2025·12:34 PM EDT | UPDATED THU, MAY 8 2025·12:48 PM EDT

Hayley Cuccinello
@IN/HAYLEYCUCCINELLO/
@HCUCCINELLO

SHARE f X in ✉

If not ODA, how else can governments secure support for digital development?

As the data and discussion above show, immediate crises, whether refugees or COVID-19, have significant effects on how donors prioritize funding. But at the same time, the technology-related divide, or best viewed as a cliff, is also fast approaching. If developed countries want to reduce migration flows and are worried about refugees, and the digital divide is growing, which is creating fewer opportunities for economic growth in developing countries, how can developing countries catch up? It's clear given the above trends that developing countries must prioritize self-reliance, looking at funding sources domestically for the bulk of their needs and relying on ODA to catalyze or support their domestic funding mobilization capacity.

The strategies presented here take varying timeframes and resources to implement. We begin with strategies that could be leveraged most quickly and end with those that will take significant time and investment. It is important to note that these ideas are not exhaustive and only offer an introduction to self-reliance strategies.

Leverage the diaspora. The sheer volume of remittances, the funds sent home by immigrants living abroad, is the number one source of funding that developing countries receive. It is three times the size of ODA and over eight times the amount of philanthropic giving.

141

As these are private flows, it's not possible for governments to direct how they are channeled, however, governments can create vehicles that are appealing to the diaspora that allow them to invest in development initiatives. Diaspora bonds are one such vehicle.

Nigeria issued its first development bond in 2017. Despite a remittance flow of $25 billion reported in 2018, the bond raised $300 million. There is much to do to raise awareness and interest in these kinds of vehicles.[241] India has had much greater success. It issued three diaspora bonds in 1991, 1998, and 2000 and raised $1.6 billion, $4.2 billion and $11.3 billion, respectively.[242]

Figure 7: Largest sources of external funding for developing countries

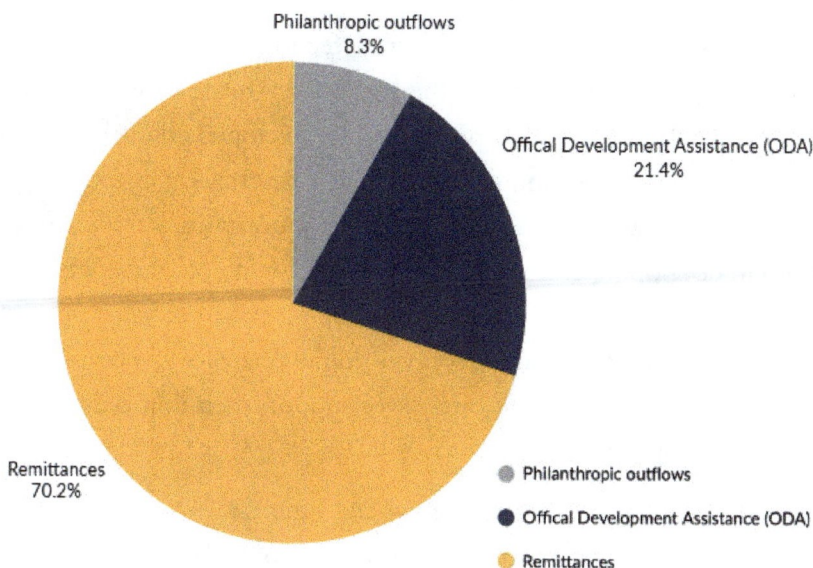

Philanthropic outflows
8.3%

Offical Development Assistance (ODA)
21.4%

Remittances
70.2%

- Philanthropic outflows
- Offical Development Assistance (ODA)
- Remittances

Source: Interaction

---

[241] Rogers, Dennis, *Diaspora bonds: An innovative source of financing?* (Parliament Observer, September 29, 2022).
[242] Nairametrics, *How diaspora bonds work and benefits* (September 20, 2019).

Knowledge transfer. Organizations like the World Bank[243] are increasingly calling themselves knowledge banks, in acknowledgement that funding alone without the knowledge that goes with it is insufficient to benefit from the digital economy. Despite the tempting alternatives from new multilateral institutions like the China Development Bank or the New Development Bank (formerly BRICS bank), where countries can secure assistance, often with limited environmental or social safeguards, the knowledge that accompanies the World Bank and similar institutions has continued to make it the go-to for countries seeking to compete in the increasingly global digital economy.

Levering the diaspora for knowledge, and not just capital, is another alternative. The International Organization for Migration (IOM) launched a dedicated program to support diaspora knowledge transfer through a program called Migration for Development in Africa (MIDA),[244] and UNDP launched a similar initiative called UNDP's Transfer of Knowledge Through Expatriate Nationals.[245]

Technical assistance through a variety of vehicles. Donors are investing in new, nimble vehicles that combine resources of multiple donors to create the depth of expertise that each donor is unable to host themselves. For example, recently, a new vehicle has been created to address the gender digital divide called the Women in the Digital Economy Fund (WiDEF), with initial support from the Gates Foundation and USAID.[246] Similar platforms are emerging for supporting governments with digital public infrastructure, such as Co-Develop.[247]

---

[243] Semuels, Alana, *Ajay Banga Wants the World Bank to Work as a 'Knowledge Bank' to Reduce Poverty* (January 11, 2024).
[244] IOM, *Migration for Development in Africa* (IOM, 2024).
[245] https://www.undp.org
[246] Global Digital Inclusion Partnership, *The Time is Now: Policy Actions to Close the Gender Digital Divide | Women in the Digital Economy Fund* (Global Digital Inclusion Partnership, November 24, 2024).
[247] https://www.codevelop.fund/

A platform to support governments to procure technology solutions for supervision, the SupTech Lab,[248] was first piloted then launched under the auspices of Cambridge University.

Another notable example is the Alliance for Financial Inclusion (AFI),[249] a membership platform for peer learning of regulators and supervisors. AFI was initially housed under GIZ, the German aid agency, with funding support from the German government and the Gates Foundation. After nearly a decade of public support, AFI is now a registered agency housed in Malaysia with a diversified funding structure including membership fees from Central Banks and Ministries of Finance, as well as some public donors such as the Ministry of Foreign Affairs in Luxembourg and the Swedish Aid agency, SIDA. AFI, Co-Develop, and several other technical assistance platforms are structured as south-south initiatives where learning is generated in developing countries for peer learning with other developing countries.

Domestic taxation. Ultimately, the long-term source of revenue for any government is its tax revenues. This is often a challenge for developing countries given the high levels of informality in their economies, the limited capacity of state institutions, and the low levels of incomes for most citizens. But generating revenue through taxation does not necessarily require income taxes. Some of the world's leading economists are now calling for what's called sin taxes.

Masood Ahmed, former head economist at the IMF, and Minouche Shafik, formerly President of Columbia University, argue that "A 50 percent increase in the price of tobacco, alcohol, and sugary drinks through higher taxes could raise $2.1 trillion for low- and middle-income countries over five years, according to the Task Force on Fiscal Policy for Health. That's equivalent to 40 percent of their public health

---

[248] https://lab.ccaf.io/
[249] https://www.afi-global.org/

spending and far exceeds official development assistance, which currently amounts to about $223 billion a year."[250]

These taxes not only help with revenue, but they also result in improved health outcomes and can offset healthcare spending. "Tax increases that raise the price of these harmful products by 50 percent would save 50 million lives over the next 50 years as well as prevent significant health problems."[251]

While there may be pushback from these 'sin' industries to such measures, public opinion generally supports these types of taxes. Surveys in Colombia, India, Jordan, Tanzania, and the U.S. have consistently shown that a majority of people support raising these taxes, particularly when health benefits are explained, and revenues are designated for public services.

The good news is that this has been tested, and it has worked in several countries. The Philippines was able to increase revenue from $1 billion in 2012 to $2.9 billion in 2022 due to sin taxes. Lithuania was able to double its tax revenue on alcohol between 2015 and 2022.[252]

Domestic capital markets. A large share of development assistance is structured as debt and not grants. Many governments are borrowing from development finance institutions (DFIs) such as the World Bank, the Asian Development Bank, the African Development Bank, and other DFIs. These loans are often in hard currencies, which can be difficult for countries to pay off given limited access to hard currencies domestically and the high variations in exchange rates.

In my own birth country of Egypt, the Egyptian pound was allowed to float freely on March 6, 2024, causing an approximate 40–60 percent depreciation in a single day—from ~31 EGP/USD to over

---

[250] Ahmed, Masood and Shafik, Minouche, *The Case for Health Taxes* (IMF, March 2025).
[251] ibid
[252] ibid

50 EGP/USD.[253] Given that over 40 percent of the country's debt is denominated in hard currencies, a weaker pound means it takes significantly more Egyptian pounds to pay each dollar of debt. Debt servicing now consumes over 56 percent of all government spending.[254] An alternative to accessing funding from international organizations in hard currencies, many countries need to invest in and promote domestic capital markets, allowing them to issue local bonds in local currencies.

Some countries have already made significant investments in their capital markets, which will mean an easier transition in this post-aid era. In 2023, Brazil issued its first sovereign sustainability bond valued at $2 billion.[255] Indonesia has issued $3.5 billion in conventional, green, and Sharia-compliant bonds.[256] Recognizing that domestic capital markets development is a long-term process, countries may need to rely on issuing public debt in global markets to support making this transition.

What next?

This is not an easy time for developing countries to fall behind in their digital development. And yet their debt burdens and shrinking development assistance funding will require more creative and catalytic ways to leverage the resources that are available. Many developing countries and some global experts see the current situation as potentially the necessary breaking point that was needed for much-needed reforms in the traditional development architecture. They note that a large amount of international development funding was not effective and possibly incentivized dependency rather than self-sufficiency.

---

[253] Egyptian Initiative for Personal Rights, *The shock of the 3rd flotation and its impact on social justice*, (EIPR, March 6, 2024).

[254] The Crisis Group, *Egypt in the Balance?* (Crisis Group, March 31, 2023).

[255] Government of Brazil, *Brazil announces first issuance of sustainable bonds* (Gov.br, November 14, 2023).

[256] World Bank, *Unlocking Growth: Developing Domestic Capital Markets for Private Investment and Jobs* (WBG, April 25, 2025).

The fourth global conference on financing for development recently took place in Seville, Spain. This conference comes amid this highly volatile and rapidly changing geopolitical landscape with many traditional ODA donors retrenching. The conference championed a renewed focus on effectiveness of aid, over the sheer volume of funding. Some of the messages emerging from this conference focused on debt relief, given the enormously high debt burdens that many developing countries are carrying in this post-Covid era. Other priorities that emerged were around creative ways that developing countries can finance their climate vulnerabilities through debt swaps and increasing taxation on polluting countries to cover the risks that poor countries face as a result of climate shocks.[257]

Mo Ibrahim, one of Africa's most successful businessmen and philanthropists, has noted that less foreign aid should push Africa to "embrace self-reliance," tapping its youth, resources, and diaspora — suggesting a shift from donor dependency to internal investment.[258] During the African Development Bank's annual summit in June 2025, several African leaders, including President Alassane Ouattara and ex-President John Mahama of Cote D'Ivoire and Ghana respectively, made similar calls for self-reliance.[259]

Some countries have already taken steps in this direction. Nigeria recently approved a U.S. $200 million additional domestic investment in its health sector, while South Africa pledged to replace PEPFAR HIV funding with domestic resources.[260] Countries like Benin, Ivory Coast, and South Africa have been issuing debt in local currencies and reducing their reliance on hard-currency borrowing.[261]

---

[257] Libby, George, *Explainer: What is the UN's development conference in Seville, and what can it achieve?* (Reuters, June 26, 2025).
[258] Mo Ibrahim Founadtion, *Financing the Africa we want* (Forum Report, Mo Ibrahim Foundation, July 2025).
[259] Yieke, Lennox, *Amid funding squeeze, Africa urged to pursue self-reliance* (African Business, June 18, 2025).
[260] Katumba, Angelo, *Rethinking Africa's reliance on foreign aid* (March 26, 2025).
[261] Libby, George, *Local debt markets could shield Africa as funding sources shrink, Moody's says,* (Reuters, June 3, 2025).

Chapter 11
Civil Society

In Chapter 8 we covered what it takes to build an inclusive and equitable digital economy. We established that without safeguards, a digital economy will be dominated by the most ruthless players, those who care about their own benefits and those who have complete disregard for segments of society who may not benefit. Worse still, what is good for a few is rarely good for the system's overall safety and health. Ensuring that the digital economy is accessible to everyone and that everyone benefits requires many stakeholders to step up. We've discussed the role of governments and regulators extensively. We discussed the role of development cooperation to help governments meet their obligations, albeit with significant limitations in light of political shifts in priorities. We've also discussed why the private sector may see it in its interest to prioritize inclusion.

Now we turn to the role of civil society. We use civil society to mean all of the other stakeholders who are not government, development donors, or the private sector. It refers to the array of actors like academia, community organizations, and international humanitarian and development organizations. It is sometimes called the third sector. It refers to both formal and informal organizations. Those that have legal non-profit, academic, or cooperative status or those that are brought together by shared purpose but may not have formal legal registration.

These actors matter because they are often closest to the communities that are being impacted; they allow those who may not have the power or voice to have representation in order to influence policy, investment, or market dynamics. In Chapter 12 we will touch on the role of individual consumers and how their choices to purchase or not purchase goods can influence markets. But here we discuss how formal or informal groups can come together to help shape policy and market dynamics. Civil society influences outcomes for low-income and underrepresented groups by providing transparency, advocating for their rights, and serving as a trusted knowledge broker.

Transparency

One of the most important functions that civil society can play is shedding light on practices that the average consumer may not be aware of. Next to the volumes of legalize that companies and governments release, individual consumers would not have the wherewithal or time to review and understand privacy policies, consent forms, user instructions, or whatever else companies use to deflect their legal liabilities. A typical American looks at 1,500 websites in a year. If that person read every privacy policy that s/he came across when accessing these websites, it would take 76 working days to go through them, according to research by The Atlantic.[262] Needless to say, individuals will rarely, if ever, have the time to do this, so consumers must rely on actors that they trust who can help them figure out which companies, policies, or initiatives can be trusted.

Civil society groups, without a profit motive or shareholders, are often perceived as independent and working in the public interest. They often take on the task of conducting the necessary research and analysis to produce relevant publications and insights that help consumers make decisions.

---

[262] Wagstaff, Keith, *You'd Need 76 Work Days to Read All Your Privacy Policies Each Year* (The Atlantic, March 6, 2012).

One of the most important players in the digital economy is Consumers International, which has over 200 local member groups across 100 countries.

Its mission is to ensure that consumers have access to safe and sustainable products and services, digital or otherwise. The organization gives voice to millions of consumers and uses its clout to help shape policies. It collaborates with governments and the private sector to make sure that consumers are not underrepresented in shaping markets.[263]

Campaigns related to the digital economy include an initiative on digital rights. Its work focuses on data protection, anti-scams, AI fairness, and advocacy in online finance. In 2023, it launched the Fair Digital Finance Accelerator, a network of consumer rights organizations in 50 low and middle-income countries that are working toward a fairer and more equitable digital economy. The Accelerator aims to enhance digital finance oversight in low- and middle-income countries and empower over 100,000 consumers.[264]

Advocacy and policy influence

At the global level, one of the most viral advocacy campaigns is Oxfam's work on inequality. Oxfam's latest inequality report highlights the fact that the richest 1 percent increased their wealth by U.S. $33.9 trillion since 2015—enough to end extreme poverty more than 20 times over.[265] In its 2024 report, it highlighted that the five richest men had doubled their wealth since 2020, while nearly 5 billion people became poorer.[266]

---

[263] Consumersinterantional.org
[264] https://www.consumersinternational.org/what-we-do/fair-digital-finance-accelerator/
[265] Rubin, April, *World's richest 1% gains $33 trillion since 2015 while inequality widens: Report* (Axios, June 26, 2025).
[266] Oxfam, *Wealth of five richest men doubles since 2020, as wealth of five billion people falls* (Oxfam Press Release, January 15, 2024).

Oxfam has done substantial advocacy around CEO pay. In May 2025, Oxfam released data on the average CEO compensation, noting that it had increased by 50 percent in real terms since 2019, compared to an increase of only 0.9 percent for the average worker. According to their data, CEO pay is now 56 times that of the typical worker.

These viral data points and messages that Oxfam puts out annually help to shape the global agenda of policymakers and thought leaders.

AP News, a wire service, regularly picks up this Oxfam inequality report, and this becomes mainstream as newspapers all around the world carry these headlines.[267] Oxfam has regularly been able to influence the agenda of the elitist forums, like the World Economic Forum's annual pilgrimage to Davos.[268]

When it comes to digital economy organizations, GSMA and the Better Than Cash Alliance play an important role in advocacy for an inclusive digital economy through their engagement with the private and public sectors. The Digital Trade Alliance, formed in 2018, is a network of global digital rights and consumer advocates that engage with trade negotiators, share research, and empower other actors to influence trade policies for equity and inclusion.[269] The Digital Impact Alliance (known as DIAL), is an advocacy organization that delivers research and evidence to advocates for inclusion in the digital economy.[270]

At the country level, many local, regional, and national organizations take on the role of influencing the national debate and the policy agenda.

In Africa, a network of organizations called the financial sector deepening trusts, which were established initially by the UK development agency (previously DFID and now FCDO), play an important role in engaging with local policymakers to raise awareness and advocate for

[267] Keaten, Jamey, *Billionaires' wealth soared in 2024, anti-poverty group says as the elites prepare for another Davos* (AP, January 20, 2025).
[268] Cox, Josie, *Oxfam Inequality Report Highlights Wealth Divide As Davos WEF Begins* (Forbes, January 14, 2024).
[269] https://dtalliance.org/about-dta/
[270] https://dial.global/

digital financial systems that are inclusive, safe, and sustainable. Many are engaged at the local level to help advise policymakers on competition policy, consumer protection, data rights, and a host of other important policy issues that help shape the digital economy.

Trusted knowledge broker

Think tanks, research and knowledge organizations, play an important role in uncovering information on policy, consumers, market players, and other stakeholders to inform the public at large. In inclusive finance, CGAP and CFI serve as trusted knowledge brokers helping donors, investors, policymakers, and the private sector understand challenges of low-income individuals and small firms and support initiatives that are most effective at addressing their challenges. For example, CGAP recently released its impact pathfinder to help market actors, policymakers, and others identify the latest evidence on what works to serve low-income individuals and small firms.[271]

Many universities play an important role. Cambridge Center for Alternative Finance, housed at Cambridge University, releases important research on fintechs, digital currencies, suptech[272] and regtech[273] solutions, and many other pertinent topics that are shaping the evolution of the digital economy. The Digital Credit Observatory at the University of California, Berkeley plays an important knowledge brokering role in the issue of digital credit and its risks.

While maintaining independence is challenging, governance is key

Just because an organization is registered as a non-profit does not automatically make it good at transparency, advocacy, or knowledge brokering. There are thousands of non-profits, and many are barely surviving. In Chapter 10 on development cooperation, we discussed the broader funding trends affecting development assistance, and these

---

[271] https://www.impactpathfinder.org/
[272] Technology solutions used for the purpose of market supervision
[273] Technology solutions used for the purpose of regulatory reporting and compliance

trends are having a major impact on the ability of civil society organizations to fulfill their mandates. Many civil society organizations have relied on donor funding for their survival. Some also rely on membership dues.

As humanitarian and development assistance funding is cut, many of these civil society organizations will need to identify other ways to fund their missions.

In the U.S., over 11,300 jobs were lost in the development space as a result of the cuts in USAID, and another 14,000 USAID jobs were also eliminated.[274] At the local level, many women and refugee-led organizations have been particularly impacted, with 80 percent of them reporting significant funding cuts.[275] Already, many organizations are looking for ways to decentralize, lower their cost structures, collaborate or consolidate with other organizations, as ways to hedge and de-risk the funding challenges that are likely to emerge in the next several years.

While the idea of diversifying income sources is appealing, there are nonetheless risks in that approach which must also be managed. Many development organizations take on non-mission-related business lines in an attempt to earn income to cover their core missions. This can work when there is strong governance, management, and policies in place to ensure that an organization's mission is not diluted.

However, it's often that these side business lines can overwhelm if not contradict the core mission.

An important non-profit in the Netherlands recently had to deal with what happens when commercial, side activities undermine the mission. The organization set up a hospitality division that rents out its conference venue on a commercial basis as a way to offset its costs and bring in additional revenue. The hospitality division agreed to host a pro-Israel organization, and the event brought some of the most extreme anti-

---

[274] Miolene, Elissa, *USAID's largest partners report furloughs for thousands of staff* (Devex, February 11, 2025).
[275] Byrnes, Thomas, *OCHA Data Confirms Scale of US Aid Cuts: 79 Million Affected, Local NGOs Hit Hardest* (LinkedIn, April 29, 2025).

Muslim and anti-immigrant speakers. The event was kept secret from staff, and only the CEO and the head of the campus were aware of the event.

Once the venue became known to participants, the information was made visible on social media platforms, and the organization's staff were contacted with inquiries. Staff immediately objected to the hosting of an event that included hate speech on their premises, but the risks of canceling the event were deemed too high by the leadership, and the event proceeded. The result was vandalism of the building, boycotting the organization by some consultants and partners, donors deciding to step away, and some students afraid to study their courses. Months after the event, the organization continues to suffer, with staff continuing to feel unsafe.

Decolonizing governance is a prerequisite to remain relevant

Misalignment with the mission is first and foremost the role of the governing bodies of any non-profit. The wrong governance model or board members can greatly undermine the mission of an organization. The case discussed above in the Netherlands was enabled precisely because the governance structure of the organization did not keep up with the core mission, programming, or evolution of the development sector. Originally founded as a colonial project, the organization retained the colonial families on the board who were initial founders.

Since its founding, the organization has received hundreds of millions of public good funding from the Dutch government, UN agencies, and a host of foundations. So, while the core work at the organization had evolved to reflect the broader trends in development cooperation and no longer relied on the interests of the original founders, its governance model had not evolved. The organization focuses its work on gender equality, social justice, and inclusion more broadly, yet the governing bodies were representative of a bygone era, made up of the original colonialists families and other elites of the Netherlands.

Organizations that serve the public interest must ensure that their governing bodies are representative of the missions they uphold. Boards must be made up of people who have the knowledge, lived experience, and skill-sets that are needed for a thriving development organization.

The board make-up at the Dutch organization was primarily Dutch, white, and corporate representatives, profiles that may be more suited for a commercial enterprise, but not a development organization in this period of rapid evolution of the sector.

Beyond the make-up of the board, the way the board operates is also central to ensuring sufficient oversight and relevance. Boards need to have direct oversight of the leadership and should have multiple sources of information on the organization's performance to fully understand the organization's influence and impact. Having transparent and accurate information is central to fulfilling this function.

What does the future hold?

Given the seismic shifts in the global funding for development, it is unclear what the future holds for the civil society sector. Many will need to remake themselves and find ways to maintain their independence and missions using not-yet-developed sustainability strategies.

At the Humanitarian Leadership Forum held in Qatar in April 2025, Amitabh Behar, CEO of Oxfam, asked the audience, made up of civil society organizations, whether they will die badly, die well, or transform.

He was raising the alarm that there is limited time left for waffling and a lack of strategic vision. Organizations that are going to survive the seismic shifts happening in the humanitarian and development landscape need to take immediate actions to reform the way they work, remove bloat, ensure they are adding value, and focus on building local capacity.

Several international development organizations, primarily large international non-profits like Oxfam and Save the Children, have signed on to the Pledge for Change,[276] where they commit to fixing colonial

---

[276] pledgeforchange2030.org

vestiges that remain embedded in their governance, management, and operational systems. They commit to ensuring they restructure their power-based relations with local organizations into equal partnerships.

They commit to change the way they communicate about people in developing countries – no longer as helpless victims -- and allow those people to tell their own authentic stories. They commit to using their privilege to influence the broader discourse on development cooperation in their own countries and beyond.

Chapter 12
The Race to Rebalance Power

In the 19th and early 20th century in the U.S., the economy was controlled by industrialists who are often referred to as the 'robber barons.' These industrialists included Rockefeller and Standard in the oil industry, Carnegie in Steel, Vanderbilt in railroads and shipping, and JP Morgan in banking and railroads. While these names are still visible in the U.S. today, the power of these industrialists is a fraction of what it was during their heyday.

Busting the industrial monopolies

A series of actions were able to break up the monopolies of the early industrialists. First and foremost was the anti-trust legislation that was spearheaded by Theodore Roosevelt. Roosevelt initiated many lawsuits during his presidency, relying on the Sherman Act. While the law was enacted in 1890, it wasn't rigorously enforced until Roosevelt's presidency, when he used it to go after companies like Standard Oil. Other antitrust regulations were enacted in 1914, notably the Clayton Antitrust Act, and the Federal Trade Commission was created to monitor and enforce competition. The Department of Commerce, created in 1903, was also an important player in addressing unfair competition. The Department of Labor, created in 1913, was important in cracking down on unfair labor practices used by the monopolies.

Clearly, the regulatory and supervisory capacity of the government was an important contributor to the break-up of the early industrial monopolies. But the regulations and the regulators were insufficient on their own. The media played an important role in shedding light on the unfair competitive labor practices, and this garnered strong public support to increase pressure on lawmakers.

The breakthrough came with the break-up of Standard Oil in 1911 when the Supreme Court ruled that the company violated antitrust laws. It was ordered to split into 34 different companies. This was the precedent that has since been the model for antitrust work. During this era, a congressional inquiry looked at the role of financial institutions and their concentration of power among a few individuals. This eventually led to the Federal Reserve Bank, which is the U.S. Central Bank.

Adapting to today's monopolies

Power today is in the hands of the BigTech companies, not the industrialists. They are not taking advantage of workers with low wages and unsafe working conditions. Instead, they attract workers with high pay, stock options, generous and comfortable campuses where workers can take time off and play sports or rest, and generous leave policies.

But their power and non-competitive tactics are nonetheless evident. It starts with money. Combined, the largest tech companies have an estimated $400 billion in cash and cash equivalents.[277] They lobby extensively, both in the U.S. and in the EU.

---

[277] https://www.macrotrends.net; (as of June 6; Apple $65.16 billion, Microsoft $75.54 billion, Amazon $101.2 billion, Alphabet $96.6 billion and Meta $78 billion).

Table 1: U.S. Lobbying expenditures in 2024

Company	Lobbying Spending (USD)	Notes	Source
Meta	$24.2 million	Highest among peers; employed 65 lobbyists, averaging one per eight members of Congress.	Opensecrets
Amazon	$17.6 million	Slight decrease from 2023; focused on various regulatory issues.	Opensecrets
Alphabet (Google)	$12.1 million	Consistent with previous year; engaged on multiple policy fronts.	Opensecrets
Microsoft	$9.5 million	Slight increase from 2023; involved in discussions on AI and other technologies.	Opensecrets
Apple	$7.7 million	Decrease from 2023; maintained a relatively lower lobbying profile.	Opensecrets

Table 2: European union lobbying expenditures in 2023

Company	Lobbying Spending (EUR)	Notes	Source
Meta	€9–9.99 million	Highest among peers in the EU; focused on digital regulation policies.	Tech.eu
Microsoft	€7 million	Engaged in discussions on digital services and AI regulations.	Tech.eu
Apple	€6.5 million	Focused on privacy and competition policies.	Tech.eu
Alphabet (Google)	€6 million	Addressed issues related to digital markets and services.	Tech.eu
Amazon	€5 million	Revised its declared spending following transparency complaints; involved in various digital policy discussions.	Euronews

The influence of BigTechs may seem inevitable, but it's not. There are already many initiatives, thinkers, and regulators who are painting a different picture of where the digital economy can go.

Rethinking competition and power of platform businesses

Similar to the robber barons, a focus on competition is essential. Competition in the digital age does not look the same as in the era of railroads. In the industrial economy, competition is often about pricing and reducing the choice of consumers. In the digital age, services are often free, so it's not about pricing.

However, consumers 'pay' in different ways, mostly through their data. So, competition policy in the digital age is mostly about regulating data; ensuring that consumers have control of their data, that there is privacy around the data, and there are limits to what companies can do with the data. Competition policy must also take into account the network effects that come with digital business models. How can consumers choose providers when they may be locked out or locked-in based on network effects? Chapter 8 on limiting monopolistic power started this conversation and gave examples of how governments are beginning to crack down on these monopolies.

As in the case of Amazon and other platform businesses discussed in Chapter 8, policy must take into account the difference between the platform and the participants on the platform. When the platform business is using its access to data to compete and undermine the participants on the platform, then there is no level playing field, and the platform firm will dominate and control the industry.

These competition issues also exist in developing countries. Many entrepreneurs in developing countries are on digital platforms to get access to clients and users. During a recent trip to Kenya, I met many drivers from several ride-hailing platforms who had turned to ride-hailing as a way to address job losses or business failures in other industries. A gentleman in his 60s decided to become a driver after losing his business during the pandemic.

He said he does everything that would be expected to make ends meet - he works over 10 hours a day, he pays his bills, and he supports his kids through school. But he can't seem to get out of debt, and he is not earning enough to compensate for his lost business. In other words, the ride-hailing gig doesn't allow him to bring in sufficient income to meet his basic needs, even though he works longer hours than a traditional job.

Also in Kenya, I met an astute business owner who was able to own multiple cars and hire drivers to work for her small business.

But despite her relative success, she found herself chasing after drivers who were not paying their car rentals. She was unsure how long she could manage her debt on the vehicles she purchased for the business. Drivers with whom I spoke, purposefully demanded cash and did not let passengers pay by card so that their transactions couldn't be captured by the platform or their lenders.

Each time I used a ride-hailing app, I wondered if these new platform jobs were the future. The platform businesses that these individuals use seem to have them trapped in a vicious cycle where they borrow to purchase their vehicles but pay such high fees to the platform business, that they can't escape their debt trap.

Consumer protections

In most countries, and for most industries, there are consumer protection agencies that monitor the marketplace to ensure that consumers are not abused. Typically, these agencies require some level of transparency and disclosure by companies. In the digital era, the consumer protection issue that needs the most attention is linked to the use of one's private data.

Data privacy

The EU's General Data Protection Regulation (GDPR), which was adopted in 2016 and came into effect in 2018, is the most comprehensive data privacy regulation in the world.

Considered landmark legislation, GDPR regulates data privacy in the EU and restricts the export of people's data outside of this economic zone. GDPR touches many aspects of the use of data including:

1. How data is processed and handled

2. Who owns the data (individuals have rights over their personal data)

3. The need for consent by users before their data is used

4. Requiring data protection as the default setting

5. Requiring consumers to be notified when their data is breached

6. Requiring large firms to have in-house data protection officers

7. Limiting the transfer of personal data outside of the EU except under strict conditions; and

8. Imposing penalties for non-compliance ($20 million or up to 4 percent of global annual turnover, whichever is higher).[278]

GDPR may not apply to all countries, but it has served as a model for many countries. Increasingly throughout the world, governments are looking at strengthening their data protection capabilities. The figure below[279] provides a snapshot of the countries in Africa that have dedicated data protection authorities (DPAs) and data privacy regulations. Many countries in West and Southern Africa have both DPAs and data privacy laws in place. Others may have one or the other or neither.

---

[278] https://gdpr-info.eu/
[279] https://privacylens.africa/infographics/

Figure 1: Countries in Africa with data privacy laws and data privacy agencies

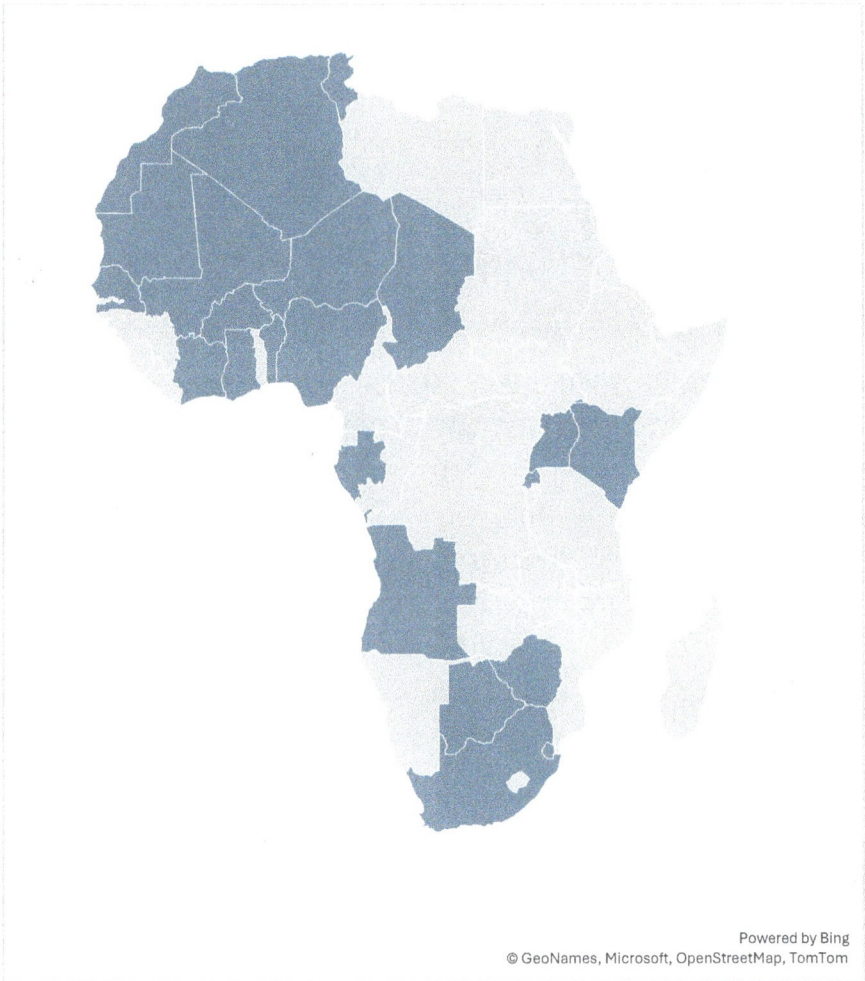

Source: Modified visual from visual produced by Mercy King'Ori and Ridwan Oleyede

Accountability and recourse

The second consumer protection issue that demands attention is accountability and recourse. In a typical digital business, there are often many players involved in what appears to be one seamless experience. In finance, there may be an agent, a bank, a FinTech, a data aggregator, and an insurer all working together. When a customer has an issue, whether it is about a mistake they made themselves or perhaps it is about fraudulent charges, who is responsible for addressing their concerns?

Recourse is a key issue that needs to be put in place so that consumers can trust the providers to resolve issues they experience. Once again, the EU is ahead of the curve on this issue. The new EU Digital Services Act[280] gives the right to consumers to challenge decisions made by platforms. An Appeals Centre was launched whose mandate is to settle "social media disputes, offering users impartial, expert, swift and cost-effective alternative to courts."[281]

Algorithmic bias

Addressing bias in algorithms is potentially the third biggest concern in the digital age. As companies collect more data and AI and machine learning are used to help make business decisions, the likelihood of unintentional bias is high. This is partly a result of the underlying data itself, which may not be fully representative of the population. For example, imagine a developing country context where women are not accustomed to using smartphones and thus have very little data trails. An algorithm designed to look at the volume of transactions an individual makes as a proxy for their creditworthiness may draw very biased conclusions that women are less creditworthy than men.

While in theory algorithms are supposed to eliminate human bias, experience to date shows that even when experts make efforts to de-bias the training data or the process itself, there are still inferior outcomes. The example of the city of Amsterdam is an interesting case in point. The city developed an AI model called Smart Check, which was built to evaluate the eligibility of welfare recipients and assess potential fraud or inaccuracies. Only those found to be high risk would receive home visits, thus potentially reduce the workload and improve the efficiency of the program.

The city worked with leading AI specialists and used every recommendation in the responsible AI playbook.

---

[280] European Union Agency for Criminal Justice Cooperation, *Digital Services Act: ensuring a safe and accountable online environment* (EuroJust, March 20, 2024).
[281] https://www.appealscentre.eu/

It ran bias tests, put safeguards in place, and obtained feedback from welfare recipients in the program. Furthermore, the system included a feature that enabled explainability, or the ability of people to see how the model produced the outcome. This is rare in algorithms, where most are considered black boxes that are hard for users to explain the results. Most importantly, it also avoided all protected characteristics like gender, nationality, or age, which could potentially lead to bias.

Table 3: Criteria used to score welfare applicants in Smart Check

Rank	Description
1	Percentage participation in welfare scheme in previous year
2	Days since last moved house
3	No-contact or no-reply appointments in previous year
4	Sum of assets
5	Days since last shift
6	Co-occupants?
7	Received benefit in previous year?
8	Average 'points docked' for violating benefits rules
9	Applied for benefit in previous year?
10	Average of gross income
11	Address in Amsterdam?
12	Single or partnered?
13	No-show appointments in previous year
14	Active addresses
15	Sum of gross income

Source: MIT Technology Review

Despite the best-in-class application of responsible AI, the city discovered that the results of the model were still biased, particularly against migrants and men. The model flagged non-Dutch applicants more often than Dutch applicants and was twice as likely to flag non-Westerners. Taking this into account, the city then re-weighted the results to correct for this bias. After going live and testing the system alongside human analysis, the algorithm was found to be lacking on two fronts: it flagged many more welfare applicants than the human-based system, and it was no more efficient than a caseworker at the task.

Ultimately, the city dropped Smart Check after multiple years, and millions of Euros were spent on it.[282]

Improving governance of public infrastructure and public goods

Who should decide how the internet is run? Who should decide how a public good of any kind is run? In today's world, BigTech companies are the ones driving most of the key decisions. When they release new technology, they may not have thought through how this technology may be harmful to society. Their philosophy, as coined by Mark Zuckerberg and used as the Facebook motto until 2014, was always 'move fast and break things.'

When the major decisions tech companies were deciding were whether the selection menu was on the left or right, perhaps these decisions were not significant enough for regulators or most people to raise concerns. But today, without oversight, technology that forms the basis of the digital economy – digital infrastructure and digital public goods - can create many risks, such as the risk of exclusion, bias, infringement of one's privacy, and limitations on the rule of law.[283] Improving the governance around public goods has become perhaps one of the most important challenges of our time.

Work is already happening to shape the governance of public goods. A UN report released in 2024 has outlined a framework for safeguards for digital public goods and infrastructure (see Box 1 below).

---

[282] Guo, Eileen, et al, *Inside Amsterdam's High Stakes experiment to create fair welfare AI* (MIT Technology Review, June 2025).
[283] Nt, Sarasvati, *Ensuring Accountability in Implementing Digital Public Infrastructure: Insights from UN's Working Group Report,* (Medianama, May 7, 2024).

Box 1 : DPI Principles

1. **Do no harm**: Harms to individuals may not be immediately obvious. A human rights-based framework should be integrated throughout the DPI life cycle to proactively and effectively assess and address any potential human rights harms and power differentials.

2. **Do not discriminate**: All individuals, regardless of their intersecting identities, should be empowered with unbiased access. Circumstances of historically vulnerable communities, marginalized groups, and those who opt out should be included in every risk assessment.

3. **Are not exclusive**: All individuals should have alternative modes (digital/non-digital) to access services enabled by DPI based on their individual capacity and resources. Modes of access should not be limiting, conditional, or mandatory — explicitly or de facto.

4. **Reinforce transparency and accountability**: DPI should be developed with democratic participation, public oversight, promote fair market competition, and avoid vendor lock-in. All partnerships should be transparent, accountable, and publicly governed.

5. **Guard by the rule of law**: DPI should be introduced with a clear legal basis and regulated by laws. Regulatory frameworks should be supported with capacity for sector-specific tailoring (e.g. health), implementation, and oversight.

6. **Promote autonomy and agency**: Ensure that everyone (especially indigenous communities with sui generis rights), on their own or with assistance, can take control of their data, promote their agency, exercise choice, and ensure their society's well-being.

7. **Foster community engagement**: All stages of the DPI life cycle should centre on the needs and interests of individuals and communities at risk. They should engage, participate at critical junctures, and actively provide feedback in an environment of transparency and trust.

8. **Ensure effective remedy and redress**: Complaint response and redress mechanisms, avenues for appeal, supported by robust administrative and judicial monitoring and review processes, should be accessible to all in a transparent and equitable manner.

9. **Focus on future sustainability**: Emphasizing foresight is a key responsibility to anticipate and limit long-term harms. For example, environmental impacts of DPI due to factors such as e-waste management policies of countries should be assessed and addressed.

Source: UN, Leveraging DPI for Safe and Inclusive Societies, April 2024

More importantly, it is necessary to discuss who needs to be at the design table. Governance of public infrastructure and public goods is not something left to the private sector or even to government alone. There is a vital role for civil society, academic institutions, experts, consumer protection agencies, and others to have a role in shaping how these important assets are governed.

Empowering consumers

Consumers today have more choices than ever. Near ubiquitous access to mobile phones, internet access, and social media platforms allows anyone, anywhere, to give recommendations and share information on companies, products, or the news. The rise in TikTok users to nearly 2 billion people in 2023 is emblematic of how people today are sourcing their information.

Figure 3: Active TikTok user globally (Billions)

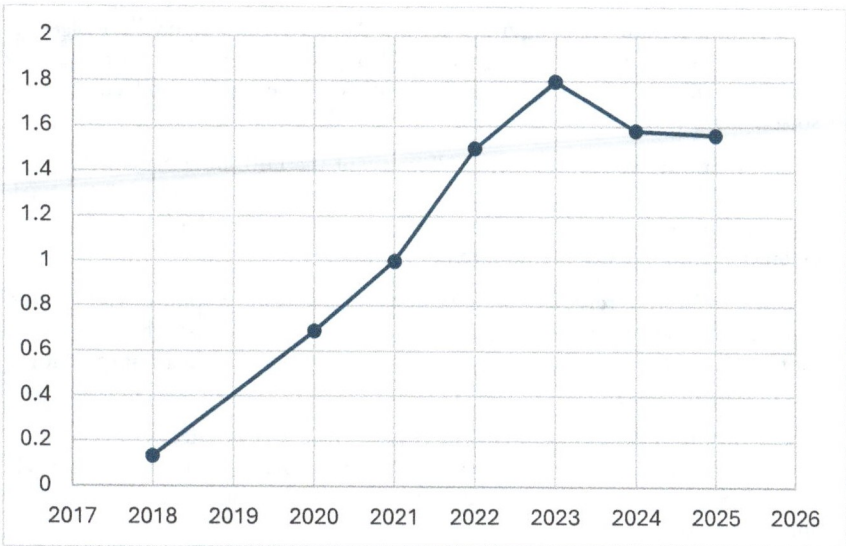

Sources: *statista, Tekrevol.com, businessofapps.com*

But power of the consumer does not just lie in individual choices, the network effects that benefit digital businesses also manifest among the users.

We have seen what the network effects can trigger. The Arab Spring was the epitome of social movements using social media to ignite people to the streets, which eventually toppled many of the authoritarian regimes that had been in place for decades.

While the outcomes may not have aligned with what these movements wanted,[284] this does not deflect the power that was garnered from citizen action using social media.

The graph below provides a developmental model of how consumer power evolves in the digital age. Initially, the internet presents an opportunity for consumers to express their demands by allowing them to choose from more options, let's call it voting with their click or pocketbook. Over time, consumers are able to add content themselves to gain their own following and traction. This shifts them from passive users to active participants in driving action.

Figure 4: Sources of consumer power in the digital age

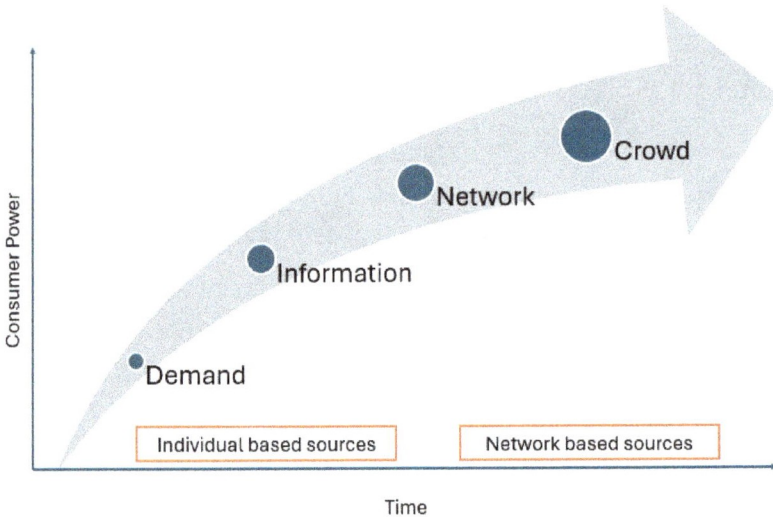

Source: Modified from Consumer Power: Evolution in the digital Age[285]

---

[284] The regimes that have taken over after the Arab Spring have often been as bad if not worse than those that were toppled, stifling freedoms and worsening the economic conditions of the countries.

[285] Labrecque, Lauren et al, *Consumer Power: Evolution in the Digital Age* (Journal of Interactive Marketing, 27(4):257–269, November 2013).

One of the most powerful tools that consumers have to influence corporate practices is boycotts and campaigns around them.

Perhaps the most well-known is the campaign against Nestle for its marketing of infant formula instead of breastfeeding, particularly in developing countries. The Infant Formula Action Coalition launched a campaign against Nestle's advertisement in the U.S. in 1977, which spread globally. Actions led to the World Health Organization releasing a new code of conduct called the International Code for Marketing Breastmilk Substitutes.[286] The campaign and new code of conduct were effective in altering Nestle's practices, which eventually agreed to abide by the code of conduct.

A more recent boycott campaign was the #DeleteUber campaign. In 2017, activists started this campaign in response to Uber's attempt to profit from a strike by the New York Taxi Workers Alliance, which was undertaken in protest of the Trump Muslim ban. The campaign was mostly spread through Twitter, and it is estimated that it resulted in over 200,000 people deleting the Uber app from their phones.[287] The campaign eventually led to the CEO's resignation and major restructuring of the leadership and internal policies at Uber.

Another important one was the #grabyourwallet campaign, which was initiated in response to Trump's 'grab them by the pussy' comment in the Access Hollywood tapes. The campaign aimed to raise awareness of Trump family businesses and encouraged consumers to boycott these companies.[288] The campaign reached nearly 1 billion impressions and led Nordstroms to drop Ivanka Trump shoes, handbags, and other products, and over 3,600 Trump branded items were dropped by online retailers.[289]

[286] World Health Organization, *International Code of Marketing of Breast-milk Substitutes* (WHO, 1981).
[287] Plumer, Brad. *Why Trump just killed a rule restricting coal companies from dumping waste in streams* (Vox, February 16, 2017).
[288] https://grabyourwallet.org/
[289] Devereux, Courtney, *#GrabYourWallet campaign is making consumer boycotts great again* (StopPress, February 28, 2017).

Another consumer power strategy is buycotts, which, as its name purports, is the act of purchasing something in support of a company.

One of the most successful such campaigns is that for Ben & Jerry's when the company announced it would stop selling its ice cream in Israeli settlements in Occupied Palestinian Territories.[290] This campaign continues to garner loyalty to Ben & Jerry's among ethically conscious consumers.

Box 2: Busting the BigTechs: The case of Google

Under the Biden Administration, the Department of Justice (DOJ) took steps to address the growing monopolistic power of the BigTechs. One of the most notable actions was the lawsuit against Google, which maintained that Google's practice of being the default search engine on browsers set up through bilateral agreements with other tech companies limited consumer choice. The fact that most consumers are overwhelmed and rely on the default settings of the technology companies is what makes default apps or settings critically important in the competitive landscape.[291]

The DOJ is asking for the termination of bilateral agreements that make Google the default search engine, demanding the spinoff of the Chrome browser, and restricting how AI is used in the search function.[292] Another lawsuit, which the DOJ won in April 2025, focused on Google's advertising business claiming its dominance allowed it to inflate prices. The ruling stated that Google "harmed Google's publishing customers, the competitive process, and, ultimately, consumers of information on the open web."[293]

The fight against the monopolistic power of the BigTechs extends well beyond the U.S. In fact, the European Union has been more aggressive and more successful in its fight against tech dominance. In 2018, the EU fined Google €4.125 billion for practices linked to the Android operating system. Google was accused of requiring manufacturers pre-installing Chrome on hardware to get

---

[290] https://www.benjerry.com/about-us/media-center/palestine-statement
[291] Hanna, Dima, *Big Tech Antitrust Scrutiny* (TALG, September 18, 2024).
[292] Michaels, Dave, *Judge Examines Steps to Limit Google's Reach in AI Arms Race* (The Wall Street Journal, May 30, 2025).
[293] Office of Public Affairs, *Department of Justice Prevails in Landmark Antitrust Case Against Google (*Department of Justice Press Release, April 17, 2025).

licensing on Google Play Store. This quid pro quo was considered abuse of its dominant market position to limit the options of manufacturers.[294]

Further afield, India has also taken positions against monopolistic power. The Competition Commission of India (CCI) targeted Google and fined it with ₹1,337.76 crore (approximately $162 million) for the pre-installed apps on Android devices.[295] The CCI also imposed a fine on Meta's WhatsApp of $25.4 million in 2024 because it shared user data with other Meta products.[296] As of this writing, there is also a Digital Competition Bill in draft form, which aims to stifle acquisitions by BigTechs intended to kill their competition.[297] Both Brazil and China have also continued to tackle BigTech dominance by reforming their antitrust regulations and fining BigTechs for anticompetitive behaviors.[298]

What's next?

The pace of change today is dizzying. It can sometimes feel that individuals have no power and that the direction of movement is overwhelmingly against social justice. The 'flood the zone' strategy by the Trump administration and the billionaires that support him want all of us to believe this. And if we do, that is indeed the direction the digital economy will go.

But the direction of change is not inevitable, and each individual has a role to play, whether that is through what they buy or don't buy, or whether it is how they organize and take action with their peers, or how they vote. Every day as digital consumers, we make important choices.

---

[294] BBC, *Google loses appeal over record EU anti-trust Android fine* (BBC, September 14, 2022).

[295] Concurrences, *The Indian Competition Commission finds that a company abuses its dominant position* (Concurrences, April 16, 2019).

[296] Reuters, *India restricts WhatsApp sharing data with other Meta entities, imposes $25.4 mln fine* (Reuters, November 18, 2024).

[297] UNCTAD, *Protecting competition in digital markets: Policy options for developing countries (*UNCTAD, December 19, 2023).

[298] Reuters, *Brazil suggests reform to tighten antitrust regulation for big techs* (Reuters, October 11, 2024).
and Campbell, Charlie, *How China Is Cracking Down on Its Once Untouchable Tech Titans* (Time, May 20, 2021).

We use certain browsers and apps, we consent to privacy agreements, and we elect officials to represent us to set the rules of the game. These choices can either reinforce a world where our data is used against us or one in which we are directing how our data is used.

Barack Obama is famous for saying that the arc of history bends toward justice. If we use a large enough lens, we can see the full arc, and we can see how our actions can continue to push toward justice, even despite the current backlash we are living through in 2025.

Chapter 13

Closing

I started writing this book in 2023, took a hiatus, then finalized it in 2025. The world in 2023 looked very different from the world in 2025.

In 2023, the world was re-emerging after the pandemic and progress was slow but consistent. Inflation was dropping and global growth was not yet pre-pandemic levels but a reasonable level at 3.4 percent.[299] Growth in China was a healthy 5.2 percent and India was roaring at 7.7 percent. Lina Khan was in charge of the Federal Trade Commission, aggressively going after BigTechs. The EU was successfully cracking down on monopolistic practices in the European Union. The EU's Digital Markets Act came into force in 2023, requiring BigTechs to comply with a suite of rules such as preventing self-preferencing, ensuring interoperability and enabling data portability. If companies did not comply by March 2024, they would face fines of up to 10 percent of their global turnover.[300]

In 2025, we started the year with Elon Musk as a shadow president to President Donald Trump, closing down USAID, slashing and burning one federal agency after another. We've seen the BigTechs all courting the Trump administration, and we've seen the Trump family issuing and aggressively investing in cryptocurrencies. And of course, we've seen Trump attacking civil rights enforcement and going after anyone who opposes him with a vengeance.

---

[299] IMF
[300] https://digital-markets-act.ec.europa.eu/index_en

Does this mean that we should resign ourselves to a digital economy shaped by the powerful elites?

A week in 2025 feels like a year at any other time in history. By the second quarter of 2025, Elon Musk was out of favor. As of May 2025, Trump had lost 128 federal lawsuits,[301] which are estimated at 66 percent of all legal cases against him. Things are still not easy and we're less than one year into this presidency, but global shifts are beginning to take shape, and it seems unlikely that the billionaires will have as much influence as they've had this past decade.

Signs of awakening by the general public are evident everywhere in the world. In the U.S., the No King protests completely overshadowed Trump's birthday celebration with a military parade. In June 2025, over 400 academics, including 31 Nobel laureates, from more than 10 countries signed a renewed "anti-fascist manifesto," warning of creeping authoritarianism and urging defense of democratic values.[302]

Germany's "Aufstehen Gegen Rassismus" and other alliances united over 500 organizations in coordinated action against fascist movements, showing coalition-building on a massive scale.[303] In the Netherlands, where I am currently living, the right wing Geert Wilders and the Partij voor de Vrijheid (PVV) withdrew from the coalition government which pushed anti-immigrant policies, leaving the country under a caretaker until an election was organized in October 2025. Many believe this was a preemptive move given the serious decline in public support that the right-wing coalition was experiencing, estimated at only 16 percent of voters.[304]

---

[301] Tillman, Zoe and Cannon, Christopher, *In Court Trump is Losing More Than He's Winning* (Bloomberg, May 8, 2025).

[302] Hendrix, Steve, *Fearing Trump academics worldwide issue anti-fascist manifesto* (Washington Post, June 13, 2025).

[303] Thomas, Mark, *Fascism in Europe Today* (International Socialism, April 18, 2019).

[304] NL Times, *Only 16% of voters still have confidence in the Dutch cabinet* (NL Times, March 19, 2025).

After the election, the right lost seats and none of the other parties are willing to form a coalition with it. The new government is yet to take shape, so it's too early to predict the outcome.

In the Netherlands and Belgium, red line protests[305] against Israeli impunity for its serious human rights abuses in Gaza are growing. Other protests are happening across Europe and the UK. Despite crackdowns on civil liberties in Western countries, students and others continue to make their voices heard against politicians who are complicit in the Gazan atrocities.

In New York, a city with the second highest concentration of Jewish residents after Israel, a candidate for Mayor, Zohran Mamdani, beat the former governor, Andrew Cuomo, in the democratic primary. Cuomo is the embodiment of the Democratic establishment with full backing of all the requisite billionaires like Bloomberg, Ackerman, Walton, Lauder, and a host of others. Bloomberg donated over $8.3 million to the Fix the City super PAC which supports Cuomo.[306] Losing the primary, Cuomo ran as an independent and the hate campaign against Mamdani, immigrants and Muslims more generally were intense. And he still lost. This election will go down in history as a beautiful example of people defeating the billions. Mamdani will be the first Muslim and first immigrant mayor in the city's history. He is also the face of the rising opposition to the billionaire class.

It's not revolution, but incremental change

This book is not about revolution. We will not change the digital economy by breaking it. We can do so by incremental changes that shift the power dynamics by making it beneficial for the digital economy to serve people, all of them. Mamdani won the Mayoral race in New York because he was out in the streets talking to regular people. He was ahead in the race because he was listening to the average person and he was mirroring back what they needed. The sheer fact that someone like him

---

[305] Al Jazeera, *Thousands attend 'red line' protest in the Hague against Israel's Gaza war* (Al Jazeera, June 15, 2025).
[306] Metzger, Bryan, *The billionaires who bet big on the NYC mayoral primary and lost* (Business Insider Nederland, June 25, 2025).